American Sterling Silver and Silver-Plated Hollowware

Other Titles in the Warner Collector's Guides Series

Available Now

The Warner Collector's Guide to
American Sterling Silver and Silver-Plated Hollowware

James H. Burke

A Main Street Press Book

WARNER BOOKS

A Warner Communications Company

Warner Books, Inc.
75 Rockefeller Plaza
New York, N.Y. 10019

w A Warner Communications Company

Printed in the United States of America

First printing, June 1982

10 9 8 7 6 5 4 3 2 1

Library of Congress Cataloging in Publication Data

Burke, James H.

   The Warner collector's guide to American
sterling silver and silver-plated hollowware.

   (The Warner collector's guides)
   Bibliography: p. 253.
   Includes index.
   1. Silverwork—United States—Collectors and
collecting. 2. Silverplate—United States—Collectors
and collecting. I. Title.
NK7112.B797 739.2'3773 80-25229
ISBN 0-446-97634-2 (U.S.A.)
ISBN 0-446-37093-2 (Canada)

Contents

How to Use This Book

The purpose of this book is to provide the collector with a visual identification guide to American sterling silver and silver-plated hollowware. Numerous books are available which describe, in detail, the work of individual silversmiths and silver companies such as the Gorham Manufacturing Company of Providence, Rhode Island; Tiffany & Company of New York City; and the Unger Brothers of Newark, New Jersey. The fifty categories in this easy-to-use guide, however, present a broader perspective, and provide even the most inexperienced collector with an overview of the wide range of silver objects available, the diversity of companies which created them, and the various styles and techniques employed by 19th- and early-20th-century silversmiths.

Four broad classifications pertain to the area of the house in which a given piece of silver was most likely to be used, or to the function it served for the individual. These broad areas include pieces for the dining table and the drawing room table; pieces for general use around the house (such as candelabra or vases); and silver accessories to be carried on the person (such as match safes) or used in the boudoir or bath (shaving accessories, brushes, etc.). Within the four major categories, objects are further subdivided by their type—bowls, pitchers, goblets, and so on.

Use of this collector's guide is designed with ease and portability in mind. Suppose you spot a silver mug that appeals to you at a flea market or in an antiques shop. Perhaps the dealer has told you the obvious: "It is an early-20th-century American mug." But is it sterling or silver plate? Who was the maker? Is its decoration common to other pieces, or unique? Was it perhaps made as a commemorative piece for a specific occasion or person? These are just a few of the questions you may want answers to.

By turning to the Color Key to American Sterling Silver and Silver-Plated Hollowware (pp. 17-48) you will find among the fifty color illustrations a photograph of a piece that bears a close resemblance to the one you are interested in—the visible characteristics, the basic shape, are similar. Under the color illustration will be found the number and name of the classification. By turning to the number and chapter heading in the body of the book which corresponds with the color photograph (i.e., 4. Cups and Mugs) you will be able to find either the identical piece or a piece very similar to it. By turning to the pages in the body of the book, you will discover, among other things, the piece's probable maker, the date and place of manufacture, a concise and detailed description of its shape, decoration, and distinctive markings, and its approximate availability (i.e., whether it is rare or common). A careful inspection of the piece itself will also tell you a great deal, since often the maker's mark and date symbol will be visible (see the section on maker's marks in the general introduction).

Each of the 420 pieces of sterling silver and silver-plated hollowware discussed in this guide is treated in a separate numbered entry containing basic information. A typical entry is reproduced on p. 9, together with a list of all the basic elements contained in each entry of the book. Most of these elements are self-explanatory, but the reader should take note of several areas.

Marked pieces: As many signed pieces as possible have been included in this guide because these furnish the most accurate documents for attribution to a particular maker; it should be remembered, however, that much 19th- and early-20th-century silver was not marked in any way.

Flatware: American flatware is not included here since it is the subject of a forthcoming volume in the Warner Collector's Series.

Price range: This is a treacherous area, so let no one fool you into thinking that any so-called price guide is a completely accurate means of determining the value of a piece of silver. Essentially, an object is worth whatever a collector is willing to pay for it, and prices can vary because of the widely fluctuating price of silver on the international money markets. This guide, therefore, offers guidelines not to price, per se, but to **availability,** based on the following considerations: (1) that the piece of silver or silver plate is in perfect or near perfect condition; (2) that marked examples are more desirable and valuable than unmarked pieces, which means that unmarked examples that are comparable to illustrations here of marked pieces would be less valuable than the range indicated by the letter code; (3) that a number of museum objects have been used as illustrations because they were readily available and provide accurate documentation. The ranges assigned to these museum pieces, however, do not necessarily apply to the particular object illustrated, but are only suggestive of the **type** of silver piece in the entry. The availability ranges suggested in this guide are coded as follows:

A—very rarely available
B—rarely available
C—often available
D—commonly available

A Typical Entry

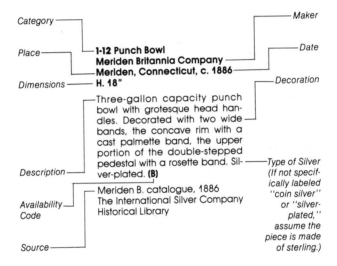

Category

Place

Dimensions

Description

Availability Code

Source

Maker

Date

Decoration

Type of Silver (If not specifically labeled "coin silver" or "silver-plated," assume the piece is made of sterling.)

1-12 Punch Bowl
Meriden Britannia Company
Meriden, Connecticut, c. 1886
H. 18"

Three-gallon capacity punch bowl with grotesque head handles. Decorated with two wide bands, the concave rim with a cast palmette band, the upper portion of the double-stepped pedestal with a rosette band. Silver-plated. **(B)**

Meriden B. catalogue, 1886
The International Silver Company
Historical Library

Introduction

Before the latter half of the 19th century the production of domestic silver was largely limited to items which were handmade by individual craftsmen. The availability of vast new sources of the precious metal, the emergence of a prosperous middle class, and the invention and acceptance of electroplated silver contributed to the widespread manufacture and purchase of various forms of silver in the United States during the 1800s. By the 1850s, with labor cheap and plentiful and silver selling for less than $1 a troy ounce, items could be readily mass-produced in a factory-like setting. As a result, extravagance became the rule. Silver began to be used for objects that had previously been made of porcelain, pottery, or a base metal.

Since the 1840s sterling pieces have been primarily machine-made, with various types of ornamentation done by hand. The initial production lines of such well-known companies as Tiffany and Gorham consisted largely of sterling. The "Elkington patent of 1840"— the process by which a base metal could be easily plated with silver—resulted in the first factories capable of producing a line of cheap, durable, and attractive silverware.

The Rogers brothers—William, Asa, and Simeon—perfected a nickel alloy that was eminently suitable for silverplating. Both William and Asa had initially worked as silversmiths with Joseph Church, making spoons and forks from "coin" silver (silver literally melted down from coins). Asa left the firm of Church and Rogers to form a partnership in 1830 with John A. Cole of Rogers and Cole, and by 1836 William, with Simeon's assistance, had become one of the first in the country to manufacture tableware of sterling silver. In 1845 Asa became a partner in the Cowles Mfg. Co., where he began experimenting with the electroplating process. Later in 1845 William and Asa became partners with J.O. Mead of Philadelphia and manufactured electroplated silverware under the title Rogers and Mead. The partnership was short-lived. In 1846 the Rogers brothers bought out the Cowles Mfg. Co. and the following year began silverplating as Wm. Rogers & Co., Hartford, Connecticut. The success of the Rogers brothers illustrates the effect which this new process had on the entire silver industry. This transition from sterling to plate production occurred throughout the country.

The largest proportion of silver manufactured for domestic use consisted of sterling and plated hollowware for the dining table. An article from 1868 rhapsodizes:

> The appearance of a dinner-table set with silver for a large party is so exceedingly splendid that we can hardly wonder that fashion has adopted this metal for her own. Nothing conveys a more vivid impression of royal magnificence and imperial state. . . . Show me the way people dine, and I will tell you their rank among civilized beings.

And this statement was made before the widespread popularity of silverware for the dining table.

The tea table was also supplied with a full complement of silver. After teaspoons, the silver teapot was usually the first item acquired. Gradually, pottery and porcelain pieces were replaced with silver, until the entire table glittered. As a writer of the 1890s so graciously described the inspiring array:

> Marshall in array, as only a woman's fingers can, the cheerful, hissing urn, the teapot with queer little old-time strainer hanging to the spout, the liberal dish of sugar lumps, the slender jug, the sugar tongs—thin, graceful, lustrous, with golden claws—the spoons attenuated through the years of honorable service. . . . Forget not the tea caddy, modern or antique, an article on which fashion just now lavishes much extravagance. Nor omit the platters bearing waferlike slices of buttered bread and cakelets.

Once the dining table and the tea table were replete with silver, attention turned to other rooms in the house. Card receivers and vases were produced by the silver-plate companies almost immediately after production began in the 1840s. Candlesticks and candelabra were found in sterling and plate in both the dining room and the drawing room. Accessories for the library desk and accessories for smokers were introduced later in the century.

Silver became popular for toilet articles during the 1890s and reached a peak of popularity during the first quarter of the 20th century, before bobbed hair and beauty parlors became common. Most of the articles were created for women, but men had their military brush sets and silver-mounted razors, strops, shaving brushes, and other barber equipment.

A study of silver catalogues—from the 1850s, when the first silver catalogues were distributed to retail stores, until the Depression in the 1930s—reveals a great deal about American social history. As the country expanded and profited economically, the variety of items offered to an eager public began to reflect the increasing affluence of the upper middle class. The Meriden Britannia catalogue of 1855, for example, offered a scant 20 different items for sale. Included, of course, were caster sets, tea sets, urns and kettles, ice pitchers, butter dishes, cake baskets, fruit stands, goblets and cups, sugar tongs, trays, candlesticks, a molasses cup, liquor mixers, and specialized ladles and spoons. All of these were silver plate, since Meriden did not produce sterling until the 1890s. By 1861, only six years later, 43 categories of hollowware were offered—80 caster sets, 7 napkin rings, as well as toast racks, spoon holders, knife rests, beer pitchers, and an item reflecting the state of acceptable manners, a silver-plated parlor spittoon.

The 1886 Meriden catalogue was the largest ever produced by the company. Its 450 pages contained page after page of tea sets, punch bowls, biscuit jars, cake baskets, berry dishes, whisk brooms, pap sets, clocks, flasks, hand mirrors, and lavatory sets. By this time the spittoon was politely called a cuspidor in an effort to impart a degree of respectability to this unlikely silver object.

Reed & Barton's most comprehensive catalogue was issued in 1884. It, too, featured silver plate exclusively, since Reed & Barton did not produce sterling until 1888. The catalogue pictured almost 3,200 separate items, many available in more than one finish and in different sizes. Many categories included over 100 variations. Listed were 194 butter dishes, 201 trays, 108 spoon holders, 163 fruit dishes, 179 casters, 188 cake baskets, 117 vases, 63 napkin rings, 55 coffee and tea urns, 81 tea services, 48 tilting ice water sets, 59 kettles, 91 cups, and 67 goblets.

In 1896 the Gorham Company distributed a small booklet of gift suggestions, with prices ranging from under 50¢ to $10. As difficult as it is to conceive of such low prices from our 20th-century perspective, there were, in fact, over 900 separate articles available for less than $10 apiece. Among the more obscure items offered as suggestions were perfume funnels, whist counters, horseradish spoons, mustache brushes, telegraph pad holders, spurs, pea spoons, gum cases, and coupon scissors. Some of these were silver plate, but a great many were also fashioned in sterling silver.

A comparison of Reed & Barton's 1912 silver-plate catalogue with their sterling hollowware catalogue offers some indication of the gap between the upper classes who bought sterling, and the majority, who had to be content with silver plate. Many articles were found in both catalogues, but such exclusive items as champagne goblets, glove stretchers, menu holders, and wine list holders were available only in sterling. Condensed milk can holders and catsup bottle holders, on the other hand, were some of the utilitarian items available only in silver plate. The decorations on silver plate tended to be more ornate, although there were extravagances in solid silver that defy description.

The style and decoration of silver follows closely the trends in the decorative arts during the 19th century, from neoclassical to Colonial Revival. The early silver manufactured in the 1850s was quite simple, a reflection of the colonial and Federal periods in the United States. Classical figures of gods and goddesses, cherubs, and naturalistic animals and animal heads were predominant motifs during the '50s, '60s, and '70s. The influence of Sir Charles Eastlake, whose **Hints on Household Taste** was published in the late '60s, was evident in the geometric designs and angular forms common in the decades that followed.

Gradually, as silver designers explored the possibilities inherent in the electroplating process, designs grew more elaborate. The factory machinery also became more sophisticated, resulting in an infinite variety of silver parts that could be combined in unlimited permutations. Once the object was formed, the decoration was added, either in the form of die-cast borders and cast decoration, or hand-cut engraving, chasing, and repoussé work. In the 1880s Gorham's preface to their hollowware catalogue listed several new methods of decoration. The transition to more elaborate embellishment is indicated by the following description of decorative techniques:

> Applied, Beaten or Hammered, Parcel Gilt, Etched, Engraved and Decorated in Color; Inlaying with Gold, Platinum, or Copper; various forms of Chasing, such as Repoussé, Flat Incise, or Intaglio, and Carved; Roller Borders in great variety, to which constant accessions are being made; Niello, a process known in the Middle Ages, in use by the earliest engravers, and which has come down to us from Russia and France.

The '80s and '90s also witnessed the widespread interest in Middle Eastern and oriental motifs, and the "Turkish corner" was a unique feature of Victorian household decoration. Art Nouveau, the graceful undulating style prevalent at the turn of the century, was particularly adaptable to silver. Simultaneously, however, there was a revived interest in 18th-century styles, and much of the silver manufactured during the early years of the 20th century was made to complement the architectural and interior designs of the Colonial Revival.

MARKS

Although the American silver industry is a direct descendant of colonial silversmithing and its English traditon, there has been no parallel attempt in America to mark silver as carefully as it has been in England. Almost any piece of English silver manufactured in the last four centuries carries five marks—the lion passant, denoting metal of sterling quality; the reigning sovereign's head; the mark of the city of origin; the date mark; and the maker's mark. In a glance an expert can identify a piece as to period and place, although for the exact date a guide to marks must be consulted.

The only mark used consistently by American silver manufacturers is the word "STERLING," though occasionally the ratio "925/1000" is used to denote sterling quality. Prior to the adoption of the sterling standard in the 1860s, most silver was coin silver of 900/1000, the ratio of silver to copper in American coins of the period. A few examples of coin silver appear in this guide since they are representative of similar pieces produced in sterling and silver plate.

Most silver companies also mark their pieces to differentiate their products from the works of other manufacturers. These marks range from the name or initials of the company, to a symbol, such as an eagle or a unicorn. Gorham, for example, uses the lion passant and the gothic "G" flanking an anchor. From 1868 until 1884 Gorham marked its hollowware with letters denoting the year of manufacture. The silver-plated child's mug illustrated in chapter 4 (see 4-6) bears the letter "Q" for the year 1884. Later, symbols were substituted for letters until the practice was discontinued in 1933. Other major companies date their work through changes in their trademarks, which usually cover a span of years. Dominick and Haff was the only major company that stamped the actual date of manufacture on its goods, and then in a somewhat disguised fashion, with the date arranged in a diamond "1 $\frac{9}{2}$ 0."

Tiffany & Co. silver can be dated by means of the various marks used since 1850. Clues to the period are provided by the name of the company, its address, and the initial of the incumbent president. Sometimes the time period during which the piece was made can be narrowed down to a five-year period (1902-07) when the president's initial "C" was used; at other times the time span can be as much as thirty-one years (1907-38) when a script "M" was used. Within this large period one can approximate a data stylistically, or determine it exactly by a presentation inscription or dating of some other kind. In addition to the regular Tiffany marks, the company used symbols to denote articles made during the years of the Columbia Exposition in Chicago in 1893, the Exposition Universelle in Paris in 1900, and the Pan-American Exposition in Buffalo in 1901.

For the most part, the larger companies making sterling hollowware used various devices to date their wares, changing the device each year. Smaller companies had shorter lives, so their wares can usually be dated simply by noting the trademark used. Other marks found on both sterling and silver plate include pattern and order numbers. In addition, retailers of stature often had their names stamped on goods at the factory.

Silver-plate companies usually marked their goods with a single stamp that incorporated the company name, its location, and the quality of the plate. The type of pattern was stamped separately, usually below the company stamp. Confusion sometimes results, however, when a pattern number such as "1850" is mistaken for a date. The collector must also be meticulous when searching for marks, since they may appear almost anywhere, particularly on the more elaborate pieces. For the most complete listing of manufacturers' marks on silver and silver plate, consult Dorothy T. Rainwater's **Encyclopedia of American Silver Manufacturers.**

Even such an extremely useful reference work as this, however, does not eliminate the need to do some detective work in the "field" of museums and shops. Marks do not always tell the whole story. In the late 19th century, for instance, a number of manufacturers produced pieces which were sold to and marked as the products of retail jewelry and silver firms. It can take some time to sort out the history of such a piece and this may involve a comparative study of typical forms and decorative styles.

Opportunities for today's collector, including the beginner, to acquire attractive and useful antique sterling and plate are considerable. Until recently, little attention has been paid to manufactured Victorian sterling and even less to its poor cousin, plate. Georgian and early American silver, however, has become exceedingly rare and, as the supply has diminished, the price has skyrocketed. Although the speculative prices of a year or two ago no longer prevail, handcrafted silver remains a luxury. Later manufactured pieces are by no means bargain-basement items, but they can be found at reasonable prices at both the major auction house and the neighborhood antique shop. And there can be no doubt but that they will appreciate in value considerably in coming years.

Color Key to American Sterling Silver and Silver-Plated Hollowware

1. Bowls

2. Water Pitchers

3. Tilting Pitchers

4. Cups
and Mugs

5. Goblets

6. Trays

7. Meat Platters

8. Entrée and Vegetable Dishes

9. Other Serving Dishes

10. Tureens

11. Sauceboats

12. Ladles

13. Bread Dishes and Cake Plates

14. Cake Baskets

15. Bonbon and Nut Dishes

16. Butter Dishes

17. Syrup
Pitchers

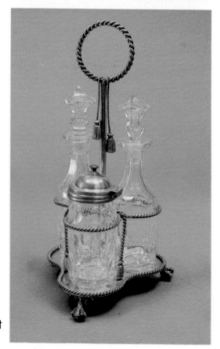

18. Cruet
Stands

19. Pickle
Casters

20. Mustard
Pots

21. Sugar Casters

22. Salt Cellars and Salts and Peppers

23. Compotes, Épergnes, and Centerpieces

24. Tazzas

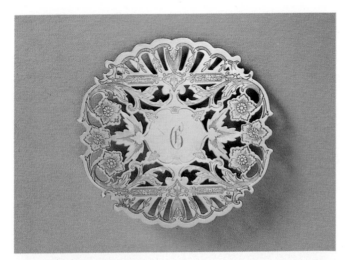

25. Protectors and Holders

26. Napkin Rings

27. Toothpick and Spoon Holders

28. Knife Rests

29. Bells

30. Wine and Liquor Accessories

31. Tea and Coffee Services

32. Teapots

33. Coffeepots and Urns

34. Teakettles

35. Sugar Bowls and Cream Pitchers

36. Tea Accessories

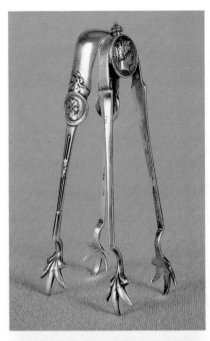

37. Sugar
Tongs

38. Candlesticks
and Candelabra

39. Flower Vases and Bowls

40. Trophies

41. Card Receivers

42. Desk Accessories

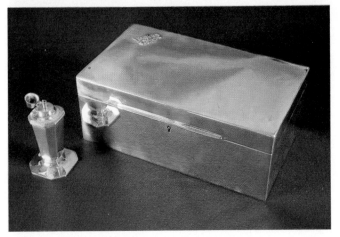

43. Smoking Accessories

44. Toilet and Boudoir Accessories

45. Hand Mirrors

46. Perfume Bottles and Containers

47. Brushes and Combs

48. Shaving Accessories

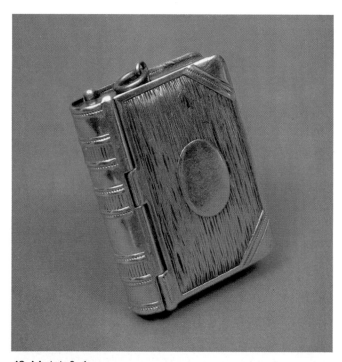

49. Match Safes

50. Boxes

I THE DINING TABLE

1 | Bowls

Bowls have been formed from almost every material known to man. The silver bowl, although not the most useful, ranks with the finest of porcelains in beauty and value, and is infinitely more durable. The silver bowl usually consists of a single basic shape. It is a concave vessel, either round or oval. Variations may include a lip that can be inverted or everted, a rim that can be regular or irregular, and a base with various forms of feet or a simple pedestal.

The fact that silver is such an excellent conductor of heat necessitates the use of silver bowls exclusively for dry or cold items. Small bowls can be used for edibles, potpourri, or flower arrangements; large bowls often function as centerpieces filled with fruit, flowers, or foliage, or as ice containers and punch bowls. A medium-sized bowl, often decorated as in 1-0, can be used at the table to serve various small fruits.

Bowls are usually decorated on the outer or inner surfaces, the height of the bowl determining the amount of surface area available for decoration. Bowls decorated on the outer surface are often engraved or chased (1-4). When decorated on the inside, the embellishment is usually at the rim and consists of a cast and applied border (1-3) or an overall repoussé decoration (1-9).

The most common silver bowl manufactured in the 20th century is the so-called Revere bowl (1-10). In the late 1700s Paul Revere used a Chinese export bowl as a model for his silver bowl. During the Colonial Revival period of the early 1900s, a reasonable copy of this design was produced in various sizes and has remained popular.

1-O Bowl (color plate)
Gorham Mfg. Company
Providence, Rhode Island, c. 1900
D. 10"

A classic fruit bowl. The foot, sides, and broad rim embossed with strawberry plants. Gilt interior. **(B)**

The Burt Collection

1-1 Bowl
Stone Associates
Gardner, Massachusetts, c. 1925
D. 9⅞"

Circular bowl on a spreading rim foot, the flaring sides alternate with broad and narrow fluting. Slightly everted rim. **(B)**

1-2 Bowl
Tiffany & Company
New York, New York, c. 1860
D. 9¼"

Circular bowl with embossed scalloped rim and chased with scrolls and foliage, supported on four cast, applied scroll feet. **(B)**

The Burt Collection

1-3 Bowl
Whiting Mfg. Co.
Providence, Rhode Island, c. 1890
D. 9"

Circular form on a molded foot with a band of stylized leaves and flowers between narrow bands of palmettes at the top. **(B)**

Private Collection

1-4 Bowl
Stone Associates
Gardner, Massachusetts, c. 1925
D. 8"

Circular bowl on a short, flaring rim foot. Divided into six sections by six vertically chased tulip-like flowers. Molded rim. **(B)**

Private Collection

1-5 Bowl
Stone Associates
Gardner, Massachusetts, c. 1925
D. 8½"

Circular shallow bowl, broadly fluted on a rim foot. **(B)**

1-6 Bowl
Carl R. Forssen
Boston, Massachusetts, 1907
D. 5⅞"

Circular shallow bowl with an inverted rim, on a pedestal with a spreading rim foot. Forssen was a silversmith with the Handicraft Shop of Boston. **(B)**

Private Collection

1-7 Bowl
Tiffany & Co., Inc.
New York, New York, c. 1930
D. 9"

Hexagonal bowl on a rim foot, the body divided into six sections by broad fluting. **(B)**

1-8 Bowl
Goodnow & Jenks
Boston, Massachusetts, c. 1900
D. 11"

Circular bowl with three harp handles. Molded, reeded banding at the base, the rim, and on the side where the top of the handle is joined to the body. **(B)**

Private Collection

1-9 Berry Bowl
Unger Bros.
Newark, New Jersey, c. 1905
D. 11"

A shallow, circular bowl; the rim decorated with naturalistic orchids; the body divided into seven sections by double fluting. **(C)**

Williams Collection

1-10 Bowl
Tiffany & Co., Inc.
New York, New York, c. 1938
D. 5"

A 20th-century adaptation of the classic 18th-century design by Paul Revere, itself based on the popular Chinese export bowl design. The modern silver bowl has a slightly everted rim, whereas Revere's prototype was straight. **(D)**

Ren's Antiques
Newtown, PA

1-11 Punch Bowl
Meriden Britannia Company
Meriden, Connecticut, c. 1877
H. 30"

A punch bowl and stand for goblets from the 1870s. The stand has six paw feet and twelve circular rests for goblets. Silver-plated. **(B)**

Meriden B. catalogue, 1877
The International Silver Company
Historical Library

1-12 Punch Bowl
Meriden Britannia Company
Meriden, Connecticut, c. 1886
H. 18"

Three-gallon capacity punch bowl with grotesque head handles. Decorated with two wide bands, the concave rim with a cast palmette band, the upper portion of the double-stepped pedestal with a rosette band. Silver-plated. **(B)**

Meriden B. catalogue, 1886
The International Silver Company
Historical Library

1-13 Punch Bowl
Meriden Britannia Company
Meriden, Connecticut, c. 1886
H. 24"

Two-and-one-half gallon capacity. Circular bowl on a tall stepped pedestal with two draped female figures seated on the second step. The two vertical bands on the steps decorated with engraved foliage. The band on the bowl rim engraved with arcs. Four female masks on the rim. Silver-plated. **(B)**

2 | Water Pitchers

The water pitcher, or ewer, was an important fixture on the dining table of the Victorian family. In the days before iced drinks and at a time when wine was served only to adults at rather formal occasions, cool spring water was the primary beverage at the dinner table. Pitchers came with and without covers, and in a variety of styles. The classic pear-shaped form is actually a larger version of the 18th-century coffeepot, with simple harp handles. In the late 19th century the pitcher gradually evolved to include more elaborate chased and repoussé decorations and fanciful scroll and double-scroll handles.

Although the double-wall tilting ice pitcher became very popular during the late 1800s (see chapter 3), it was costly, so the single-wall pitcher continued to be manufactured. In fact, the sterling silver pitchers made during the period from 1870 to 1910 are some of the finest examples of silver manufacture. The basic size and form of a pitcher made an ideal base for the art of the silver designer (2-8, 2-17).

2-0 Water Pitcher (color plate)
Goodnow & Jenks
Boston, Massachusetts, c. 1890
H. 6¾"

Octagonal-shaped, slightly flared pitcher with engraved wreath in the center on each side and swags around the top. Four cast paw feet with acanthus leaves above joined to four sides of the body. Reeded banding at the rim. Wooden C-shaped handle. **(B)**

Private Collection

2-1 Pitcher
Ball, Black & Company
New York, New York, c. 1850
H. 13"

Baluster-shaped pitcher chased and repoussé with floral sprays. Scrolls and foliage surround a central cartouche with a presentation inscription. The domed lid with a floral and foliage finial. Four open-work splayed feet. The handle and spout decorated with vines, leaves, and buds. Made by Eoff & Shepherd, New York City, for Ball, Black & Company. **(B)**

2-2 Pitcher
Gorham Mfg. Company
Providence, Rhode Island, 1908
H. 11"

Vase form with chased and repoussé raspberry canes, leaves, and fruit on the body. Cast raspberry canes and leaves applied to the shaped handle. **(B)**

2-3 Pitcher
Reed & Barton
Taunton, Massachusetts, c. 1868
H. 12"

Ovoid body on a stepped spreading rim base. Cast applied spout with cornucopia. Scroll handle with medallion. Stepped lid with a cupid finial. Greek key border at the rim and on the lid. Silver-plated. **(B)**

Reed & Barton Collection

2-4 Pitcher
Gorham Mfg. Company
Providence, Rhode Island, 1868
H. 8¼"

Ovoid body decorated with three cast stag heads and engraved geometrical designs. The short neck decorated with an undulate band. The square handle with a medallion decoration. **(B)**

The Burt Collection

2-5 Water Pitcher
Dominick & Haff
Newark, New Jersey, 1884
H. 8⅛"

Pear-shaped body with swirling flutes at the top under a boldly beaded border. Entire body repoussé with flowers and foliage. Leaf pattern on C-shaped handle. Bold beading outlining the edge of the spout. **(B)**

2-6 Pitcher and Waiter
Gorham Mfg. Company
Providence, Rhode Island
c. 1900
H. 11"

Ovoid body on a quatrefoil base with a conforming square waiter. The rims of the pitcher and the waiter undulate. The whole decorated with flowers and foliage. Scroll handle and matte finish typical of the "Martelé" works of the period created entirely by hand from sheets of silver. "Martelé" (after the French word for 'hammered'), was introduced by William C. Codman, Gorham's English-trained chief designer. Each piece was unique. **(B)**

The Burt Collection

2-7 Water Pitcher
Jacobi & Co.
Baltimore, Maryland, c. 1890
H. 10"

Pear-shaped body with repoussé and chased acorns, oak leaves, and ivy vines on a stippled ground. Satyr mask with garlands under the spout. Cast rustic scroll handle, rim foot. **(B)**

Lyndhurst Corporation
New York, NY

2-8 Water Pitcher
Tiffany & Co., Inc.
New York, New York, c. 1870
H. 9¼"

Baluster shape with horizontal banding in various styles. A row of beading below the lip, below that a broad rosette band between narrow geometric bands. The primary decoration on the body is a broad band of elephants in various poses. A fluted lower band completes the decoration of the body. Rim foot with three geometric bands. Cast handle with fluting and reeding and a cast elephant's head at the lower joining of the handle to the body. **(B)**

Lyndhurst Corporation
New York, NY

2-9 Water Pitcher
Samuel Kirk
Baltimore, Maryland, c. 1840
H. 10¼"

Pear-shaped with chased and re-poussé flowers and foliage on a matte ground. Domed circular foot similarly decorated. Applied cast spout in the form of a bearded man. Scroll handle with leafage at top and bottom. **(A)**

Lyndhurst Corporation
New York, NY

2-10 Pitcher
Charles W. Hamill & Co.
Baltimore, Maryland, c. 1884
H. 9"

Round pitcher tapering sharply to a stepped rim foot pedestal. The shoulder with a broad band of embossed foliage, flowers, and figures. Cast scroll handle and flat pouring rim. Silver-plated. **(C)**

Collection of Mr. & Mrs. Theodore Rockafellow
New Britain, PA

2-11 Pitcher
Tiffany & Co., Inc.
New York, New York, c. 1920
H. 9¼"

Classic shape with a helmet top. The only decoration consists of reeding at the lip, where the neck joins the body, where the body joins the pedestal, and on the rim foot and angular handle. **(D)**

2-12 Ewer
Samuel Kirk & Son
Baltimore, Maryland, c. 1855
H. 14¼"

Vase form with a flared lip, the body with chased and repoussé flowers, the neck ringed with vines and grapes. Each side with an Old World building in repoussé. Tall angular handle with a ram's head. Flaring pedestal base with repoussé flowers. **(A)**

Lyndhurst Corporation
New York, NY

2-13 Ewer
Tiffany & Co., Inc.
New York, New York, 1893
H. 17⅝"

Vase-shaped ewer with applied handle terminating in clusters of grapes, applied head of Bacchus beneath the spout. A repoussé frieze of dancing cherubs and satyrs bordered by grapevines above a repoussé band of swirling acanthus and grapevines. Made for exhibition at the 1893 World's Columbian Exhibition in Chicago. **(A)**

Private Collection

2-14 Ewer
Tiffany & Company
New York, New York, c. 1855
H. 9½"

Vase-shaped ewer with a helmet top on a narrow neck. The body ovoid on a flared pedestal base. The handle consists of a cast bird with another bird perched on the rim. **(A)**

The Burt Collection

2-15 Pitcher
Reed & Barton
Taunton, Massachusetts, c. 1867
H. 13"

Cylindrical, tapered covered water pitcher. Cast finial and harp handle, reeded body with engraved floral decoration beneath the spout. Silver-plated. **(C)**

Private Collection

2-16 Ice Pitchers
Meriden Britannia Company
Meriden, Connecticut, c. 1855
H. 12"

Pitchers with identical tapered cylindrical forms, one with chased scenery, including a windmill, one an early example of the "Vintage" pattern. Silver-plated. **(C)**

2-17 Pitcher
Gorham Mfg. Company
Providence, Rhode Island
c. 1901
H. 8¾"

Bulbous body with a short neck and lobed octagonal base. An overall chased and repoussé decoration of leaves and daisies. The lip and open scroll handle composed of fluted leaves with crinkled edge. Gilt interior. A superb example of Gorham's "Martelé" line. **(B)**

Lyndhurst Corporation
New York, NY

2-18 Pitcher
John B. Jones Co.
Boston, Massachusetts, 1838
H. 11¼"

Pear-shaped with chased and repoussé flower-and-leaf decoration. Cast rustic handle and spreading rim foot. Part of a presentation set inscribed to Captain William W. Peirce from the Charlestown City Guards, September 21, 1838. (For other pieces from this set see 5-1 and 6-0.) **(A)**

Private Collection

2-19 Water Pitcher
Tiffany & Company
New York, New York, c. 1865
H. 9⅜"

Classic shape with a helmet top, the body enriched with an egg-and-dart band. Flared circular pedestal base and a harp handle. **(B)**

2-20 Ewer
George B. Sharp, for Bailey &
   Company
Philadelphia, Pennsylvania
c. 1848
H. 16⅝"

The narrow neck separated from the ovoid body by a fluted border. The body decorated with repoussé rococo scrolls and flowers. Fluted shell-like support in repoussé above a circular foot. Rustic grapevine scroll handle. **(A)**

M.H. deYoung Memorial Museum San Francisco, CA

3 | Tilting Pitchers

By the 1850s a series of patents had been granted for double-wall ice pitchers. These early pitchers were freestanding and had two metal walls with an air barrier between to insulate and retard the melting of the ice. Later the inner wall was coated with porcelain to avoid what some people thought was a metallic taste imparted by the metal.

By the late 19th century a frame was added so that the freestanding pitcher could be suspended, allowing cool ice water to be obained with the touch of a finger. The pitcher was fashioned with bars on the sides which fit into the frame, enabling it to tilt. Like most inventions, the tilting pitcher became more elaborate over the years and ultimately the frame was supplied with either hooks on which to hang cups, or small platforms attached to the frame on which cups or goblets could stand (3-1). Often a waste or slop bowl was added (3-2). A tilting pitcher full of ice water subsequently became standard equipment on the dining room sideboard or buffet of the late 19th century.

The advent of modern refrigeration and easy availability of ice made the double-wall tilting ice pitcher obsolete, although the single-wall pitcher eventually returned to widespread use. Today the tilting form is highly prized and in use again at parties, where it can be used for either hot or cold drinks.

3-0 Tilting Pitcher (color plate)
Meriden, Britannia Company
Meriden, Connecticut, c. 1910
H. 19" (pitcher); H. 5" (cup)

Tilting ice water pitcher in an openwork stand with a domed base on four scroll feet. Stationary hoop handle reeded at the top for a better grip. The cannister-shaped pitcher with cast applied handle and spout. The body decorated with engraved flowers and foliage. Matching gilt-lined goblet on attached circular platform. Silver-plated. **(C)**

Ren's Antiques
Newtown, PA

3-1 Tilting Pitcher **Pairpoint Mfg. Co.** **New Bedford, Massachusetts** **c. 1885** **H. 23"**	**3-2 Tilting Pitcher** **Reed & Barton** **Taunton, Massachusetts, c. 1884** **H. 18" approx.**

Cannister-shaped pitcher supported in a frame with two goblet stands at the front. The whole decorated with Japanese motifs of

Porcelain-lined ice water pitcher. The surface hammered with a pearl finish. Two goblets stand on the stationary heart-shaped frame. Silver-plated. **(C)**

bamboo, birds, spiders, webs and foliage. Double-domed lid with cast openwork finial and scroll handle on pitcher. Stand has a double rod handle. Silver-plated. **(C)**

Lyndhurst Corporation
New York, NY

Reed & Barton catalogue, 1884

3-3 Tilting Pitcher
Meriden Britannia Company
Meriden, Connecticut, c. 1886
H. 18" approx.

Canister-shaped tilting pitcher in a simple frame with a platform for two conforming goblets. Cast applied spout and scroll handles. The base of the frame and the pitcher decorated with broad bands of repoussé flowers and masks. Satin finish. Silver-plated. **(C)**

Meriden B. catalogue, 1886
The International Silver Company
Historical Library

3-4 Tilting Pitcher
Meriden Britannia Company
Meriden, Connecticut, c. 1890
H. 21½" (pitcher); H. 6⅛" (goblets)

Cannister-shaped pitcher suspended in a frame decorated with cupids picking fruit. Matching goblets and slop bowl with swirled fluting and borders of fruit and flowers. Domed lid with an urn finial. Silver-plated. **(C)**

Private Collection

3-5 Tilting Pitcher
Meriden Britannia Company
Meriden, Connecticut, c. 1886
H. 20" approx.

Cannister-shaped pitcher on a stationary frame with openwork sides. The base holding two goblets and a slop bowl insert. The frame decorated with birds and flowers. The base, goblets, and neck of the pitcher are chased with a leaf design. The body decorated with chased palm fronds. The frame handle a gothic arch. Silver-plated. **(C)**

Meriden B. catalogue, 1886
The International Silver Company
Historical Library

4 | Cups and Mugs

The cups and mugs of the 19th century are adaptations of much earlier designs. During the 17th century handleless cups known as tumblers were popular, and until the 19th century their primary decoration consisted largely of simple fluting and embossing.

The invention of electroplating made it possible for almost every child to own a cup or mug, and these became traditional christening and birthday presents for children (4-14). Although small (averaging less than three inches in height), they were designed to be particularly appealing to children. Animals, birds, flowers, and children are often depicted on the sides of the cups (4-11), and the handles are frequently embellished with kittens, birds, or floral designs (4-7). Children's cups and mugs from the 19th century are highly collectible today. They make an ideal gift for the small child, just as they did 100 years ago.

Silver mugs and silver-plated cups and saucers were made for adults, but the adult versions often became decorative cabinet pieces, since most adult beverages were unsuitable for drinking out of silver. An exception was the adult silver mustache cup, designed to keep the mustache out of the liquid in the cup, which served as a welcome and useful present for the man of the 19th-century family. (See also chapter 48, Shaving Accessories.)

4-O Mug (color plate)
Reed & Barton

Taunton, Massachusetts, c. 1890
H. 5¼"

Tapered cylindrical form slightly flared at the rim. Plain body, the only decoration consists of a cast harp handle with the head of a crowned king as a finial. The balance of the handle richly chased. Silver-plated. **(C)**

Reed & Barton Collection

4-1 Mug
Tiffany & Co., Inc.
New York, New York, c. 1880
H. 7"

Tall, tapering cylindrical mug on a spreading rim foot. Rosette border where the top of the D-shaped handle meets the body; fluted and foliate border at the base enclosing the middle design of goldfish and seaweed in the Japanese style. **(A)**

The Burt Collection

4-2 Christening Cup
Maker unknown
c. 1910
H. 2¾"

Baluster-shaped cylindrical cup with a reeded rim foot and a reeded rim. Stylized leaf decoration on the lower half of the body; scroll strap handle with bellflowers on each side. **(C)**

4-3 Mug
Marked Braverman & Levy
San Francisco, California, c. 1875
H. 3½"

Cylindrical cup with scroll handle. Circular cartouche surrounded by engraved flowers and foliage. Narrow vertebrate band at the base. Marked "Braverman & Levy/ S.F. CALA/English Sterling." [Braverman & Levy may have been the retailers.] **(C)**

Private Collection

4-4 Mug (left)
Robert Rait
New York, New York, c. 1845
H. 3⅝"

Cylindrical mug with beaded bands at the rim and base. Scroll handle. Decorated with a buxom woman drinking from a cup in an oval cartouche surrounded by repoussé vines and flowers. **(A)**

Mug (right)
Gorham Mfg. Company
Providence, Rhode Island, 1868
H. 4"

Tapering cylindrical mug in the "Medallion" pattern with an angular scroll handle. Interlaced single band at the base. Decorated with a classical head in a small oval cartouche surrounded by an engraved pattern of hearts and swags. **(B)**

The Burt Collection

4-5 Mug (left)
Dominick & Haff
Newark, New Jersey, 1879
H. 3⅝"

Cylindrical mug with a C-shaped handle. Geometric band at the base. The upper half engraved with figures of children and the legend "Girls and Boys Come Out to Play." **(C)**

Mug (right)
Tiffany & Co., Inc.
New York, New York, c. 1930
H. 3⅜"

Cylindrical mug on a rim foot with a C-shaped handle. Upper third of the body decorated with a schoolhouse scene. **(C)**

The Burt Collection

4-6 Mug
Wood & Hughes
New York, New York, 1876
H. 3¼"

Cylindrical mug with undulate leafy bands at the rim and base. Figural handle. An oval cartouche flanked by engraved flowers and foliage. **(B)**

4-7 Mug (left)
Simpson, Hall, Miller & Co.

Wallingford, Connecticut, c. 1880
H. 3¾"

Baluster-shaped mug on a spreading rim foot. Top quarter of the body is plain and separated from the bottom by a reeded band. Scroll handle with a rabbit perched on top. Silver-plated. **(C)**

Mug (right)
Meriden Britannia Company
Meriden, Connecticut, c. 1875
H. 3"

Cylindrical mug with a broad foliate band at the base. A crouching cat on top of the handle peers down at a bird sheltered inside the handle at the bottom. Silver-plated. **(C)**

Private Collection

4-8 Mug
Reed & Barton
Taunton, Massachusetts, c. 1884
H. 3"

Slightly convex cylindrical cup with a C-shaped handle. The body decorated with a cartouche surrounded by engraved flowers and foliage. Silver-plated. **(C)**

4-9 Child's Mug
E.G. Webster & Son
Brooklyn, New York, c. 1905
H. 2½"

Convex cylindrical mug with scroll handle. Decorated with cast Art Nouveau poppies and leaves. Silver-plated. **(D)**

4-10 Cup
Gorham Mfg. Company
Providence, Rhode Island
c. 1890
H. 3¼"

Cylindrical neck on a bulbous base with stylized leaf decoration. Rim foot and harp handle with fluting on the inside of the handle. Silver-plated. **(D)**

Private Collection

4-11 Cup
Wilcox Silver Plate Co.
Meriden, Connecticut, 1876
H. 3¼"

Cylindrical cup on a spreading rim foot. The foot decorated with a band of urns, foliage, and birds. Angular handle with masks on both sides of the angle. Body decorated with a cherub swinging in a lush background of foliage. Silver-plated. **(C)**

Private Collection

4-12 Funeral Cup
Kronheimer Oldenbusch Co.
New York, New York, c. 1900
H. 2⅛"

Convex cylindrical cup with forget-me-nots on the top of C-shaped handles. Applied cast shield with initials and dates "1897-1910." Silver-plated. **(C)**

Collection of Mr. & Mrs. Theodore Rockafellow
New Britain, PA

4-13 Cup
Meriden Britannia Company
Meriden, Connecticut, c. 1885
H. 3½"

Cylindrical gilt-lined cup. Top half slightly concave, the lower half bulbous with a hammered background and floral decoration. Silver-plated. **(D)**

4-14 Baby Mug
F.B. Rogers Silver Co.
Taunton, Massachusetts, 1883
H. 2"

Cylindrical mug with a turned, everted lip. Cast hollow scroll handle. Engraved border of scrolls at base and "BABY" engraved on the body. Silver-plated. **(D)**

Private Collection

4-15 Child's Mug
A.R. Justice Co.
Philadelphia, Pennsylvania, c. 1885
H. 2⅚₁₆"

Cylindrical mug with a harp handle. Beaded border at the rim. Silver-plated. **(C)**

4-16 Teacup and Saucer
Wilcox Silver Plate Co.
Meriden, Connecticut, c. 1880
H. 2¾"

Gilt-lined teacup, bright cut with stylized flowers and foliage. Rectangular cartouche with geometric design and initials. Saucer decorated in quadrants with stylized leaf border. Silver-plated. **(B)**

Author's Collection

5 | **Goblets**

The modern goblet is a direct descendant of the 16th-century standing cup, one of the most important articles to be found at the banquet tables of nobles and royalty. While the original standing cups ranged from twelve to twenty inches in height, goblets of the 19th century were used individually at the table and are perhaps a third the size of their 16th-century prototypes.

A goblet or pair of goblets often accompanied the tilting pitcher (see chapter 3). Goblets were originally intended for wine, but never became popular because of the widespread notion that silver imparted a metallic taste. They are commonly decorated with chasing, embossing, and engine turning.

Large goblets were often used for trophies and prizes, although the 20th century saw the manufacture of silver goblets for water and stemmed silver glasses for cocktails and liqueurs.

5-O Goblet (color plate)
Reed & Barton
Taunton, Massachusetts, c. 1890
H. 5⅝"

Ovoid body and a narrow flared lip, decorated with a narrow chased band. The tall pedestal on a stepped, flared base. Silver-plated. **(B)**

The Reed & Barton Collection

5-1 Goblet
John B. Jones Co.
Boston, Massachusetts, 1838
H. 6"

Ovoid cup with egg-and-dart band at the rim. Repoussé and chased floral and foliage decoration. Stepped base. Part of a presentation service (see also 2-18 and 6-0). **(A)**

Private Collection

5-2 Goblet
Fisher Silversmiths, Inc.
Jersey City, New Jersey, c. 1940
H. 6¹¹/₁₆"

Flared cup with everted lip on a flared stem, set on a domed base. **(D)**

5-3 Cup
The Stieff Company
Baltimore, Maryland, c. 1930
H. 6½"

Flared cup with an everted rim and gilt interior. The stem flares to a spreading rim foot. **(D)**

5-4

5-5

5-6

5-4 Goblet
Meriden Britannia Company
Meriden, Connecticut, c. 1860
H. 7"

Ovoid cup with a molded rim.
Decorated with pendant tassels
and swags. The tall stem on a
slightly domed foot. Silver-plated.
(C)

Private Collection

5-5 Goblet
Meriden Britannia Company
Meriden, Connecticut, c. 1880
H. 5½"

Ovoid body with engraved floral
and foliage design on a matte
ground, surrounding a polished
shield. Set on a short stem and flaring base. Silver-plated. **(C)**

Private Collection

5-6 Goblet
Middletown Plate Co.
Middletown, Connecticut
c. 1875

H. 6¾"

Barrel-shaped cup with floral decoration between narrow geometric bands. Short stem on a domed base with a spreading rim foot. Silver-plated. **(C)**

Private Collection

**5-7 Goblet
E.G. Webster & Bros.
Brooklyn, New York, c. 1875
H. 6⅞"**

Slightly flared cup with engraved floral and fan decoration above three narrow bands of palmettes and rosettes. Thin stem on a stepped circular base. Silver-plated. **(C)**

Private Collection

**5-8 Pair of Goblets
Benjamin Mayo**

Newark, New Jersey, c. 1870
H. 7"

Flared cups with everted rims. Decorated with classical heads in cartouches; framed with urns, swags, and pendants. The stems grasped by draped putti on a four-stepped base. Silver-plated. **(B)**

Private Collection

5-9 Pair of Goblets
Manhattan Silver Plate Co.
Lyons, New York, c. 1898
H. 6⅜"

Identical flared cups with rounded bottoms. Tall stems on rim feet. Decorated with foliage and scroll cartouches. Silver-plated. **(C)**

Collection of Mr. & Mrs. Theodore Rockafellow
New Britain, PA

 | **Trays**

6 | Trays

The 19th-century silver tray was used primarily for the tea and coffee service. Trays are generally rectangular or round, although the later years of the century saw the popularization of a fan shape that fits closely to the carrier's body at the waist. A tray loaded with a tea service is heavy and the handles are closer to the body on such a tray are closer to the body and thus provide a more stable grasp (6-7).

Decoration on trays necessarily had to be flat, so they are mostly chased or engraved, often with elaborate patterns or scenes.

The Colonial Revival saw the return of the oval tray popular in the 18th century. The shaped tray, although practical, was abandoned in the early 20th century. The use of small round trays, or waiters, did, however, become popular in the 20th century.

6-0 Presentation Tray (color plate)
John B. Jones Co.
Boston, Massachusetts, 1838
L. 14⅛"

Oval tray engraved with rococo decoration of leaves and scrolls and an egg-and-dart trim at the edge. Four shallow scroll supports. (See also 2-18 and 5-1.) **(A)**

Private Collection

6-1 Tray
Ball, Tompkins & Black
New York, New York, c. 1840
L. 14⅜"

Rectangular tray with a narrow, raised rim. The outer edge gad-rooned. The center engraved with flowers and foliage. **(A)**

Private Collection

6-2 Waiter
Tiffany & Company
New York, New York, 1860
D. 12"

Circular waiter on four decorated, splayed feet. Convex, beaded edge. A circular engraved band surrounds the monogrammed center. **(B)**

The Burt Collection

6-3 Tray
Tiffany & Co., Inc.
New York, New York, c. 1890
D. 12"

Circular, hand-hammered tray with a broad rim decorated with chased daisies. **(B)**

The Burt Collection

6-4 Tray
Maker unknown
c. 1920
D. 10¼"

Circular tray with a broad rim and a scalloped edge decorated with flowers and scrolls. Rim separated from the center section by a pierced feather decoration. Center engraved with scrolls and flowers. Silver-plated. **(C)**

Private Collection

6-5 Tray
Reed & Barton
Taunton, Massachusetts, c. 1884

Rectangular, chased waiter available in four sizes: 20", 22", 24", and 26". Gadrooned border. Silver-plated. **(B)**

6-6 Tray
Rogers, Smith & Co.
Meriden, Connecticut, 1898
L. 16⅝"

Child's highchair tray, the lip decorated with a border of scrolls. Monogrammed. Silver-plated. **(B)**

Collection of Mr. & Mrs. Theodore Rockafellow
New Britain, PA

6-7 Tray
Meriden Britannia Company
Meriden, Connecticut, c. 1886
L. 28"

Tray shaped to conform to the
body. The outer rim shaped and
highly chased. The inner border
decorated with flowers and foliage. A circular central medallion.
Silver-plated. **(B)**

Meriden B. catalogue, 1886
The International Silver Company
Historical Library

6-8 Tray
Gorham Mfg. Company
Providence, Rhode Island, 1887
L. 33½"

Massive oval tray with handles at both ends. The handles decorated
with cast applied masks of female heads with elaborate headdresses.
The edge of the tray is decorated with a gadrooned border and the
center section engraved with a broad oval design of classic heads,
scrolls, and palmettes. Trays made with the same die and handles, but
with different borders and engraved centers, were made in silver
plate. This example, in solid silver, is unique. **(A)**

6-9 Hotel Tray
Gorham Mfg. Company
Providence, Rhode Island, c. 1910
L. 10¼"

Hotel ware tray. Double-stepped rim with narrow, fluted outer rim.
Silver-soldered. Silver-plated. **(D)**

7 | Meat Platters

The meat dish was introduced late in the 17th century in England and
consists of an oval form ranging from ten to thirty inches in length. For
the grandest household there might be a set of six in various sizes.
These 18th-century meat dishes were made with a simple gadrooned
border; the bottom was slightly concave inside so that the juice
gathered in the center.

The well-and-tree platter succeeded the meat dish in the 19th century, but did not entirely supplant it. It is called "well and tree" because the arrangement of the channels draining toward the well at
one end resemble a tree trunk and its branches. The well-and-tree
platter is necessarily footed to accommodate the deep well into
which the juices flow. The embellishment on these platters is generally limited to the simple gadrooned borders common on the early prototypes.

7-0 Well and Tree Platter (color plate)
International Silver Co.
Meriden, Connecticut, c. 1900
L. 16⅜"

Oval platter in the "Camille" pattern. Broad rim, the outer edge decorated with a floral band. The tree with four branches. The platter on four
splayed feet. **(D)**

Ren's Antiques
Newtown, PA

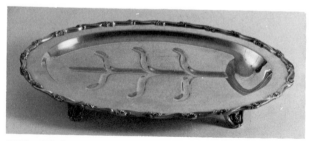

7-1 Meat Platter

Tiffany & Co., Inc.
New York, New York, c. 1940
L. 18"

Oval meat platter with a narrow rim and a reeded edge. **(D)**

Private Collection

7-2 Meat Platter
Towle Silversmiths
Newburyport, Massachusetts
c. 1915
L. 14"

Oval meat platter with two reeded handles and reeded outer rim. Also available in 16" and 18" lengths. **(C)**

Towle catalogue, c. 1915

7-3 Meat Platter
Whiting Mfg. Co.
Bridgeport, Connecticut, c. 1915
L. 18" approx.

Oval platter with a broad rim decorated with flowers and treillage, and vines trailing toward the center well. **(C)**

Whiting catalogue, 1914

7-4 Well and Tree Platter
Bernard Rice's Sons
New York, New York, c. 1920
L. 18"

Rectangular well and tree platter with rounded corners. The outer edge gadrooned. Four splayed feet. A three-branched tree. Silver-plated. **(D)**

Author's Collection

7-5 Well and Tree Platter
International Silver Co.
Meriden, Connecticut, c. 1930
L. 18¼"

Oval well and tree platter in "Sylvia" pattern, the broad rim edged with rose-patterned scrollwork. Four splayed feet, three-branched tree. **(D)**

Private Collection

---

8 | Entrée and Vegetable Dishes

Entrée and vegetable dishes in silver and silver plate are two of the most handsome items made for the dining table. Although there are meat platters which are labeled entrée dishes in the catalogues of the late 1800s, the common form is an oblong or oval deep dish with an equally deep cover and a removable lock handle. The latter enables the cover to be used as an auxiliary serving piece when a cover is not required to keep the food warm. The average size of an entrée dish is eleven or twelve inches in length; matching vegetable dishes are generally three-quarters that size, sometimes with covers, but usually lacking a stand.

Entrée and vegetable dishes are engraved, chased, and repoussé in decoration, but tend to be fairly simple in contrast to the extravagent designs common on less serviceable pieces. The type of food served in the dishes dictated smooth surfaces and rounded corners to facilitate cleaning. Elaborate decoration might be used along the rim of the dish, on the handles, the stands, or the feet and legs.

Covered entrée dishes often were sold with frames from which the dish could be suspended over a spirit lamp to keep the contents hot. Another form of stand used hot water to keep the dish warm. Entrée dishes, with or without stands, are extremely useful today for buffets and casual entertaining.

8-O Vegetable Dish (color plate)
Krider & Biddle
Philadelphia, Pennsylvania, c. 1865
L. 12³/₁₆"

Oval vegetable dish with rounded bottom. Applied cast border with female figures in relief in oval medallions at both ends. Smaller medallions at the sides with bees in relief. **(B)**

Author's Collection

8-1 Vegetable Dish
Tiffany & Company
New York, New York, c. 1860
L. 11³/₄"

Oval, covered vegetable dish with the detachable handle removed. Greek key band on the rim. **(B)**

Private Collection

8-2 Vegetable Dish
Gorham Mfg. Company
Providence, Rhode Island, 1869
L. 12½"

Shallow oval dish with grotesque mask handles. Spreading pierced foot. Beaded edge. **(A)**

The Burt Collection

8-3 Vegetable Dish
Gorham Mfg. Company
Providence, Rhode Island, 1871
L. 11⅜"

Oval dish on a spreading rim foot, two ring handles. The cover with a detachable lion handle and four scroll feet. Cover (with handle detached) may be used as a second dish. **(A)**

The Burt Collection

8-4 Pair of Vegetable Dishes
Gorham Mfg. Company
Providence, Rhode Island, 1891
L. 10½" (each)

Pair of shaped, oval, covered vegetable dishes with oval finials and scroll handles. Spreading reeded rim feet. Dish rims decorated with scrolled bands. **(B)**

The Burt Collection

8-5 Vegetable Dish
Towle Silversmiths
Newburyport, Massachusetts, c. 1915
L. 9"

Oval vegetable dish, the bottom slightly lobed. The rim decorated with cast shell and scroll border. The cover with a shell and C-scroll handle. Also available in a 13" length. **(C)**

8-6 Vegetable Dishes (top left and right)
Meriden Britannia Company
Meriden, Connecticut, c. 1885
L. 11" approx.

The top two covered vegetable dishes are identical in shape, but with different decoration. The left with fluting, the right with flowers and foliage. Silver-plated. **(C)**

Vegetable Dish (lower left)
Meriden Britannia Company
Meriden, Connecticut, c. 1885
L. 12" approx.

A dish of hammered metal with a detachable lock handle. Silver-plated. **(C)**

Vegetable Dish (lower right)
Meriden Britannia Company
Meriden, Connecticut, c. 1885
L. 13" approx.

An oval covered dish; stepped domed cover with a finial. The dish raised on four, tall cast feet. Silver-plated. **(C)**

Meriden B. catalogue, 1886
The International Silver Company Historical Library

8-7 Vegetable Dish
Barbour Silver Co. (International Silver Co.)
Hartford, Connecticut, c. 1910
L. 10″

Oval, covered vegetable dish. The top with detachable lock handle decorated with acanthus. Silver-plated. **(D)**

Author's Collection

9 | Other Serving Dishes

Included in this category are a few of the specialized dishes that Victorian designers created for a single, sometimes esoteric, purpose. The asparagus dish (9-4), for instance, is suitable only for serving that vegetable, and was a form first worked in porcelain. Similarly, the openwork dishes in 9-1 were likely suitable only for dry foodstuffs such as bread, toast, or biscuits. The cheese dish with a rat perched on the rim (9-3) would have lost its humor if used for another purpose. A cracker bowl, on the other hand, is a cracker bowl only because it was labeled as such by the manufacturer, and would have functioned appropriately on many other serving occasions.

The 20th-century porringer (9-2) is a revival of a very popular 18th-century form. Porringers were also made in pottery and pewter, silver being the rarest form.

Some other serving dishes pictured in the catalogues of the late 1800s included fish dishes, terrapin dishes, baked potato holders (in wood and silver plate), buckwheat plates, cutlet dishes, and lobster dishes.

9-O Sweetmeat Dish (color plate)
Dominick & Haff
Newark, New Jersey, 1899
L. 8"

Die-stamped dish profusely decorated with foliage, flowers, and birds
in the William Morris tradition. **(B)**

Author's Collection

9-1 Dish (left)
Tiffany & Co., Inc.
New York, New York, c. 1905
L. 7¾"

Shaped, pierced oblong dish with a gadrooned border and four ball
feet. **(C)**

Dish (right)
Tiffany & Co., Inc.
New York, New York, c. 1905
D. 5¹³⁄₁₆"

Circular pierced dish with flared, scalloped sides and a gadrooned
border. **(C)**

The Burt Collection

9-2 Porringer
Maker unknown
c. 1915
L. 7" (with handle)

Bulbous dish with everted rim and
a pierced flat handle. **(C)**

The Burt Collection

9-3 Cheese Dish (detail of rim)
Gorham Mfg. Company
Providence, Rhode Island, 1879
L. 8¼"

Oval cheese dish with narrow outer band enclosing a broad en-graved arc band. The center engraved with a bird. A naturalistic sculptured rat sits on the rim. **(A)**

The Burt Collection

9-4 Asparagus Dish
Tiffany & Co., Inc.
New York, New York, c. 1915
L. 14"

Shallow, rectangular asparagus dish with chamfered corners and pierced liner. **(C)**

The Burt Collection

9-5 Terrapin Dish (detail of leg)
Gorham Mfg. Company
Providence, Rhode Island
c. 1865
L. 15"

Oval dish with applied scroll handles. The four pedestal feet rest on the backs of turtles. **(A)**

The Burt Collection

9-6 Olive Dish
Towle Silversmiths
Newburyport, Massachusetts, c. 1915
L. 9½"

Oval dish with a broad, flaring, openwork wire border in a classic scroll design. **(D)**

9-7 Relish Dish
Dominick & Haff
Newark, New Jersey, c. 1925
L. 11½"

Shaped oval dish with a bellflower border. Classical motifs at both ends. Circular depression in the center for a covered glass relish dish. **(C)**

I. Freeman & Son
New York, NY

9-8 Biscuit Jar
Reed & Barton
Taunton, Massachusetts, c. 1884
H. 10"

"Rich Decorated China" jar in the
Imari tradition, set in a holder with
a bail handle and four ball feet.
Silver-plated. **(C)**

9-9 Pickle Dish
Meriden Britannia Company
Meriden, Connecticut, c. 1877
L. 10" approx.

Shallow, shaped oval dish with two handles on an oval base with four
openwork feet. The interior engraved with flowers and foliage. **(C)**

Meriden B. catalogue, 1886
The International Silver Company Historical Library

10 | Tureens

Tureens are used principally for soup, although there are other
popular entrées that contain a great amount of liquid and could be
served most practically from such a vessel. The name is said to derive

from the apocryphal story that the 17th-century Marechal de Turenne of France, without proper equipment in the field, once used his helmet to hold soup. The story may well be true since the marshal was the son of Henri, duc de Bouillon.

The tureen is covered to keep soup warm and the cover is notched so that a ladle can be left inside for the server's convenience.

The various styles of tureens are, in general, quite simple. The basic configurations are the low bulbous rococo form and the neoclassical boat-shaped form. The former is often decorated with scroll feet and an elaborate finial; the flaring form lends itself to ornamentation (10-3). The tureen in the neoclassical style is usually decorated simply with strap handles at the ends and simple fluting or reeding (10-1).

10-0 Tureen (color plate)
Reed & Barton
Taunton, Massachusetts, c. 1873
L. 16¼"

Oval body on four foliate feet. Two twisted rope handles and a finial handle. The cover with two concentric engraved bands and a cartouche surrounded by foliage. Silver-plated. **(B)**

Reed & Barton Collection

10-1 Tureen
Peter L. Krider
Philadelphia, Pennsylvania, c. 1850
L. 12⅛"

Bulbous oval body on a spreading pedestal foot. The lower half of the body and the cover are boldly fluted. Cast scroll handles. **(A)**

The Burt Collection

10-2 Tureen
Dominick & Haff
Newark, New Jersey, 1882
L. 13⅜"

Oval, pear-shaped body on a spreading rim foot, decorated with chased and repoussé flowers, dragonflies, and cattails on a hammered ground. The domed cover similarly decorated. Cast loop finial handle. Two handles. **(A)**

Private Collection

10-3 Tureen
Whiting Mfg. Co.
Providence, Rhode Island, c. 1886
L. 11"

Pear-shaped oval body on four paw feet. Applied cast handles. The body and the concave cover boldly fluted. **(B)**

The Burt Collection

10-4 Tureen
William Gale & Son
New York, New York, 1856
L. 14½"

Oval tureen on a spreading rim foot pedestal. Greek key and beaded borders at the base, rim, and surrounding the handle. Scroll handles at the ends and a classical wreath as the finial handle. **(A)**

Private Collection

10-5 Tureen
Meriden Britannia Company
Meriden, Connecticut, c. 1885
L. 14" approx.

Oval body on a stepped spreading foot. Bull's heads for handles and a naturalistic standing bull as the finial handle atop the conical cover. Bold floral patterns within a geometric border. Silver-plated. **(B)**

Meriden B. catalogue, 1886
The International Silver Company
Historical Library

11 | Sauceboats

The sauce or gravy boat accompanied almost every course at the dinner table during the mid-to-late-19th century. Such a vessel was indispensable for sauce accompanying a shrimp cocktail, for tartar sauce with a fish course, for mayonnaise in a cold salad, for hot gravy or sauces to accompany meats, or for fruit and chocolate sauces to go with dessert. The boat is commonly used in conjunction with a small platter, which is sometimes separate, but more often soldered to the bottom for safety purposes.

Sauceboats vary in length from six to eleven inches. The pouring lip is usually broad, providing an easy flow for whatever liquid is being served, although thick sauces will often be accompanied by a ladle (see chapter 12). Boats with attached platters are usually set on a spreading foot, while the freestanding boat that is passed on a tray is often three-footed in one of the traditional styles: ball, hoof, snake, etc.

The sauceboat in the shape of a fish (11-8) is a unique variation on the traditional forms. It seems likely that it was designed to serve tartar sauce with the fish course. The sauce may have been poured from the front opening (fish's mouth) or ladled from the top.

11-0 Pair of Sauceboats (color plate)
William Gale & Son
New York, New York, 1856
L. 7½"

Open boat form on a stepped pedestal base; decorated with beaded borders at the rim, the base of the boat, and the base. Double-scroll handles with foliage. **(A)**

The Burt Collection

11-1 Sauceboat
Dominick & Haff
Newark, New Jersey, 1885
H. 5¼"

Symmetrical, oval sauceboat with pouring spouts at both ends and a scroll and bellflower handle on the side. Waiter with a central circular depression and similar decoration. **(B)**

I. Freeman & Son
New York, NY

11-2 Sauceboat
Gorham & Company
Providence, Rhode Island
c. 1855
L. 10"

Classic boat shape on a circular pedestal. The scroll handle forks at the crest. Made of coin silver,

but typical of the forms produced
in sterling and silver plate. **(B)**

The Burt Collection

11-3 Sauceboat with Waiter
Tiffany & Co., Inc.
New York, New York, 1924
L. 9½" (waiter); L. 6¼" (boat); L. 8" (ladle)

Open boat form with a wide lip. Scroll handle. Circular waiter and
ladle to match. **(B)**

The Burt Collection

11-4 Sauceboat
Towle Silversmiths
Newburyport, Massachusetts, c. 1915
L. 11"

Open boat form with scroll feet, scroll rim, and double-scroll handle.
Similarly decorated oval tray. **(C)**

11-5 Sauceboat
Towle Silversmiths
Newburyport, Massachusetts, c. 1915
L. 11"

Open boat form with scroll feet. The strap handle and the edges of the
boat and the tray are gadrooned. **(C)**

11-6 Sauceboat
Lebkuecher & Co.
Newark, New Jersey, c. 1900
H. 4¼"

Open boat form on three cast, applied shell feet. Double C-scrolled
handle. **(C)**

I. Freeman & Son
New York, NY

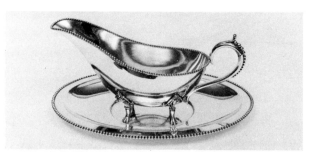

11-7 Sauceboat
Meriden Britannia Company
Meriden, Connecticut, c. 1890
L. 9¾"

Open boat form on four paw feet. The scroll handle, the edge of the waiter, and the rim are beaded. Silver-plated. **(C)**

Collection of Mr. & Mrs. Theodore Rockafellow
New Britain, PA

11-8 Sauceboat
Gorham Mfg. Company
Providence, Rhode Island, 1891
L. 6"

Sauceboat in the form of a fish, elaborately chased with scales; the tail forming a loop handle. **(A)**

Private Collection

12 | Ladles

The silver ladle is the ne plus ultra in a long line of iron, brass, copper, and wooden ladles. Ladles are made in sizes ranging from two inches long for miniature sauce tureens, to the grand punch ladles so popular in the 18th and 19th centuries. In terms of size, the gravy ladle is the most common—usually about six inches in length—with a graceful curving handle and a slightly oval bowl. The ladle for berries or fruit is often pierced to allow water to drain off.

The punch ladle is a lobed oval with pouring lips at either end. Due to silver's conductive properties, a wooden handle is a prerequisite for hot-punch ladles, although silver could be used for iced drinks. Occasionally the ladle bowl is shaped like a shell or some other form found in nature.

12-O Ladle (color plate, left)
Gorham Mfg. Company
Providence, Rhode Island, c. 1920
L. 13"

Small punch ladle with an oval, shaped bowl. The handle decorated with clusters of flowers. **(C)**

Ladle (color plate, center)
R. Wallace & Sons Mfg. Co.
Wallingford, Connecticut, c. 1930
L. 17½"

Punch ladle, the oval, shaped bowl decorated with clusters of grapes. The handle in Wallace's "Grand Colonial" pattern with a trifid end. **(C)**

Ladle (color plate, right)
Gorham Mfg. Company
Providence, Rhode Island, c. 1885
L. 13¼"

Soup ladle with a round bowl. The broad flat handle in Gorham's "St. Clair" pattern. **(B)**

The Burt Collection

12-1 Ladle
Wood & Hughes
New York, New York, c. 1865
L. 15⅛"

Punch ladle with a curved cylindrical handle. The handle decorated at the end with a Pharaonic head and scrolls, attached to the oval bowl with a palmette and supporting scrolls. Made of coin silver, but typical of the forms produced in sterling and silver plate. **(A)**

Lyndhurst Corporation
New York, NY

12-2 Ladle
Gorham Mfg. Company
Providence, Rhode Island, c. 1870
L. 11"

Square hollow handle with engraved geometrical decoration at the end of the handle and circling the oval, notched, gilt-lined bowl. **(B)**

12-3 Two Ladles
Gorham Mfg. Company
Providence, Rhode Island
c. 1860
L. 12½" (top); L. 12¾" (bottom)

Pair of ladles, the reeded handles terminating with medallions of classical heads. **(B)**

The Burt Collection

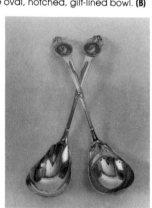

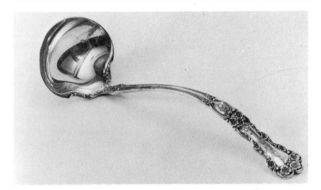

12-4 Ladle
Gorham Mfg. Company
Providence, Rhode Island, c. 1930
L. 10½"

Oyster ladle with a gently curving, shaped handle, the upper half of the handle decorated with buttercups. **(D)**

The Burt Collection

12-5 Pair of Ladles
R. Wallace & Sons Mfg. Co.
Wallingford, Connecticut, c. 1930
L. 6" (gravy ladle); L. 5½" (sauce ladle)

A sauce ladle with round bowl and a gravy ladle with oval bowl, both in Wallace's "Grand Colonial" pattern (see 12-0, center). **(D)**

12-6 Ladle
Whiting Mfg. Co.

Providence, Rhode Island, 1880
L. 7"

Small punch ladle with curving rod handle and a broad flat finial chased with scrolls. **(B)**

The Burt Collection

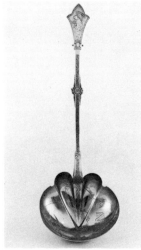

12-7 Ladle
Gorham Mfg. Company
Providence, Rhode Island
c. 1885
L. 13"

Punch ladle with a chased strap handle, the trifid finial showing a Japanese maiden carrying a fan and parasol. The bowl scalloped, shaped, and engraved in the Japanese style. **(A)**

Lyndhurst Corporation
New York, NY

12-8 Ladle (left)
Tiffany & Co., Inc.
New York, New York, c. 1870
L. 7½"

Ladle with round shallow bowl, the handle engraved with bellflowers and a cartouche with initials. **(B)**

Ladle (right)
Reed & Barton
Taunton, Massachusetts, 1895
L. 7½"

Gravy ladle with a round bowl, the handle and bowl with beading and scrolls in the "La Marquise" pattern.

The Burt Collection

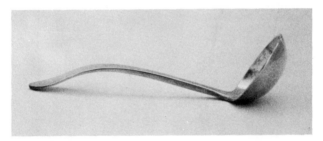

12-9 Ladle
David Carlson
Gardner, Massachusetts, c. 1930
L. 5"

Sauce ladle with a thin, pointed handle. An austere neoclassical design typical of the handwrought work of the '20s and '30s. **(C)**

Author's Collection

13 | Bread Dishes and Cake Plates

The 1890s introduced the widespread popularity of the small shallow oval tray for bread and slices of cake, such as pound cake. An even smaller bread plate, intended for only one or two slices, was also produced. They were manufactured in both sterling and silver plate and are usually lightweight and simple in design, indicative of pieces made during the Colonial Revival period. These forms continued to be manufactured throughout the 20th century and serve the same purpose today as they did when first introduced.

Cake plates also date from the days of the Colonial Revival. They are simple plates about twelve inches in diameter, suitable for holding a whole layer cake or just slices. These plates are successors to the ubiquitous cake basket (see chapter 14), which fell out of favor in the late 1890s with the return to colonial simplicity. The borders are often pierced, which makes them both decorative and inexpensive, since the amount of silver used was lessened. Cake plates were quite light-weight, and ideally suited for passing sandwiches or cakes at teatime.

13-O Bread Plate (color plate)
Gorham Mfg. Company
Providence, Rhode Island, 1877
D. 12"

Footed plate with three concentric bands, the outer two reeded, the inner band a geometric design of triangles. Between the outer two bands, in raised letters, appears the legend "GIVE US THIS DAY OUR DAILY BREAD." **(B)**

Private Collection

13-1 Cake Plate
Tiffany & Co., Inc.
New York, New York, c. 1900
D. 10¾"

Cake plate or salver with a reeded pie-crust rim in the neocolonial style. **(C)**

The Burt Collection

13-2 Cake Plate
Tiffany & Co., Inc.
New York, New York, c. 1902
L. 9"

Cake plate with two pierced geometric borders separated by a thin band. **(C)**

The Burt Collection

13-3 Bread Tray
Meriden Britannia Company
Meriden, Connecticut, c. 1910
L. 12½"

Oval bread dish divided into quadrants by embossed pendant bell-flower decoration. The border pierced in a vertical pattern. **(C)**

Private Collection

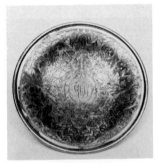

13-4 Cake Tray
Homan Manufacturing
Company
Cincinnati, Ohio, c. 1905
D. 9⅝"

Circular plate with elaborately engraved leaf and scroll design superimposed on a geometrical ribbon outline. Silver-plated. **(C)**

Collection of Mr. & Mrs. Theodore Rockafellow
New Britain, PA

13-5 Cake Plate
Van Bergh Silver Plate Co.
Rochester, New York, c. 1915
D. 10"

Cake plate with a wide, pierced scroll border surrounding openwork. Silver-plated. **(C)**

Collection of Mr. & Mrs. Theodore Rockafellow
New Britain, PA

13-6 Bread Tray
Rogers, Smith & Co.
Meriden, Connecticut, c. 1915
L. 12"

Long, oval bread tray with flared sides and beaded edge. Silver-plated. **(C)**

13-7 Bread Tray
Rogers, Smith & Co.
Meriden, Connecticut, c. 1915
L. 12"

Long, oval bread tray with flared sides and foliate edge. Silver-plated. **(C)**

13-8 Bread Tray
Manhattan Silver Plate Co.
Lyons, New York, c. 1900
L. 12¾"

Oval bread tray with openwork border of poppies and stems. Silver-plated. **(C)**

Collection of Mr. & Mrs. Theodore Rockafellow
New Britain, PA

14 | Cake Baskets

The cake basket was an extremely popular form during the latter half of the 19th century. As the 20th-century bride despairs on receiving twenty-four silver pepper mills, so the bride of the 1880s must have blanched when presented with an excess of cake baskets. One firm alone offered 188 different styles in the 1870s.

Cake baskets were first made in the late 18th century and were one of the most elegant dishes available for the household. They were characterized by a grace that only partially carried over to the more elaborate confections of the late-Victorian period, when the attempt to create something unique for the buying public resulted in what might politely be called overdecoration. The form, nevertheless, was attractive and consisted of a shallow, round or oval bowl, either pierced or solid, with splayed or rim feet, and often with an elaborate bail handle. Almost any cake basket of the period found in good condition is usable today for a variety of purposes, including carrying cake.

14-O Cake Basket (color plate)
William Adams
New York, New York, c. 1830-1835
L. 16¼"

Oval lobed body on an oval pedestal. Anthemia bands on the inside of the rim and at the base. Cast bail handle with leaves and fruit. **(A)**

Private Collection

14-1 Cake Basket
Wood & Hughes
New York, New York, 1865
L. 13½", H. 13"

Shaped oval basket on a stepped pedestal foot. The edge decorated with scrolls and beading. The open bail handle terminating in a ball finial.

The Burt Collection

14-2 Cake Basket
Tiffany & Co., Inc.
New York, New York, 1908
L. 9"

Hexagonal, vertically pierced basket on a hexagonal base. Pierced quatrefoil rim. Strap handle. **(B)**

The Burt Collection

14-3 Cake Basket
Reed & Barton
Taunton, Massachusetts, c. 1865
L. 10⅛"

Shallow oval basket on a pedestal foot. Greek key border inside the body. Pierced outer border. Ribbon twisted bail handle. Silverplated. **(B)**

Reed & Barton Collection

14-4 Cake Basket
William Rogers Mfg. Co.
Hartford, Connecticut, c. 1890
L. 11¾"

Shallow oval basket on four scroll feet. The inside engraved with scrolls. Similar scrolls decorate the open bail handle and the shaped rim.

Silver-plated. **(C)**

Collection of Mr. & Mrs. Theodore Rockafellow
New Britain, PA

14-5 Cake Basket (top)
Meriden Britannia Company
Meriden, Connecticut, c. 1855
L. 10" approx.

Lobed form on scroll feet. Basket decorated with leaves. Silver-plated. **(B)**

Cake Basket (center)
Meriden Britannia Company
Meriden, Connecticut, c. 1855
L. 10" approx.

Form similar to the basket above, the only decoration consisting of scrolls around the inside base. Silver-plated. **(B)**

Cake Basket (bottom)
Meriden Britannia Company
Meriden, Connecticut, c. 1855
L. 12" approx.

Irregular oval form on a pedestal foot. Twisted wire bail handle. Silver-plated. **(B)**

Meriden B. catalogue, 1855
The International Silver Company
Historical Library

14-6 Cake Basket
Meriden Britannia Company
Meriden, Connecticut, c. 1885
L. 12" approx.

Shallow rectangular basket on a round base with four splayed feet, the whole elaborately engraved. Shaped bail handle. Silver-plated. **(C)**

Meriden B. catalogue, 1886
The International Silver Company
Historical Library

15 | Bonbon and Nut Dishes

Small decorative dishes suitable for mints, nuts, and small candies have been popular for years. Individual dishes used on the dining table rose in popularity with the decline of the elaborate épergne, which had served the same purpose—providing guests with sweets after dinner. A great many bonbon dishes were manufactured during the Art Nouveau period; their size made them reasonable in price, both in sterling and silver plate.

These dishes featured a wide variety of styles and forms ranging from the simple dish in 15-2, to the elaborate pierced dish raised on a dolphin stem (15-9). The basket-like form in 15-4 also features a bail handle for easy passing, while the dish in 15-6 is formed with two depressions to accommodate two kinds of candy or nuts. Larger dishes were suitable for use in a drawing room or for passing at the dining table (see chapter 9).

15-0 Bonbon Dish (color plate)
Unger Bros.
Newark, New Jersey, c. 1900
D. 7½"

A shallow, circular dish with an open border of naturalistic orchids and stems. **(B)**

Collection of The Newark Museum
Newark, NJ

15-1 Bonbon Dish
Unger Bros.
Newark, New Jersey, c. 1900
D. 7"

Circular compote with wide border of lacy openwork. Flared pedestal on a stepped dome base. **(B)**

15-2 Bonbon Dish
Tiffany & Co., Inc.
New York, New York, c. 1905
D. 3¼"

Round dish with a triangular depression. The border decorated with flowers in the Art Nouveau style. **(C)**

Williams Collection

15-3 Bonbon Dish
Wood & Hughes
New York, New York, c. 1860
L. 7½"

Lobed oval dish on a flaring stepped pedestal. A bird perches on the scroll handle. Made of coin silver, but typical of the forms produced in sterling and silver plate. **(A)**

The Burt Collection

15-4 Bonbon Basket
Unger Bros.
Newark, New Jersey, c. 1900
H. 4"

Shaped openwork basket on a reeded rim foot. Reeded bail handle. **(C)**

Collection of The Newark Museum
Newark, NJ

15-5 Pair of Bonbon Dishes
Gorham Mfg. Company
Providence, Rhode Island, 1879
5⁵⁄₁₆" square (each)

Identical square dishes with reeded borders. The bottoms engraved with birds. **(A)**

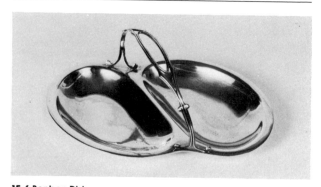

15-6 Bonbon Dish
Unger Bros.
Newark, New Jersey, c. 1900
L. 7¼"

Double dish with fixed handle forked at both ends and separated in the middle. **(B)**

Collection of The Newark Museum
Newark, NJ

15-7 Bonbon Dish
Tiffany & Co., Inc.
New York, New York, c. 1940
D. 4¾"

Round, stylized leaf shape. C-shaped handle with bold beading. **(C)**

15-8 Bonbon Dish
Victor Silver Co.
Derby, Connecticut, c. 1905
W. 7½"

Hexagonal broad-rimmed dish with a design of crocus and entwined stems. **(C)**

15-9 Bonbon Dish
Friedman Silver Co., Inc.
Brooklyn, New York, c. 1908
H. 5"

Round, pierced leaf pattern dish with a dolphin stem on a stepped pedestal. Silver-plated. **(C)**

Collection of Mr. & Mrs. Theodore Rockafellow
New Britain, PA

**15-10 Bonbon Dish
Meriden Britannia Company
Meriden, Connecticut, c. 1900
D. 5⅛"**

Circular pierced dish on four cast, applied paw feet. Everted rim. Silver-plated. **(C)**

Collection of Mr. & Mrs. Theodore Rockafellow
New Britain, PA

**15-11 Pair of Nut Dishes
Tiffany & Co., Inc.
New York, New York, c. 1872
L. 4½"**

Scallop-shell dishes on three rustic feet. The handles with classical relief heads flanked by holly sprigs and pine cones. **(B)**

16 | Butter Dishes

America in the 19th century might well have been called the land of milk and honey—and butter. Recipes of the period called for large amounts of butter, and it was used unsparingly on pancakes, fresh breads, hot biscuits, and vegetables. In the home, wooden molds were used to shape the butter and decorate it suitably for the butter dish in which it was to be presented at the table. In these covered dishes the round mound of butter sat on a perforated drainer that collected the water that might sweat out. Crushed ice could also be placed beneath the drainer to prevent melting in hot weather.

The cover helped protect the butter from flies and dust, and also served to keep it cool. Usually the cover was simply removed while a portion of butter was taken, but later dishes feature bell covers that slip up and down on frames or can be rolled back. Illustration 16-7 shows a butter dish with a jointed handle on the bell cover. After lifting the cover, a horizontal turn fixes it in place until the serving is finished. The entire butter dish apparatus is often set on ball or splayed feet.

Commercially made butter and the use of modern refrigeration techniques ended the widespread use of the old-fashioned butter dish. Individual packaging of butter by the pound and quarter pound made this traditional utensil obsolete. Illustration 16-10 shows two butter dishes used for commercial sizes; 16-3 illustrates a dish from the 1920s used for butter balls.

16-O Butter Dish (color plate)
Duhme & Company
Cincinnati, Ohio, c. 1860
H. 8¼"

Circular butter dish on a stepped pedestal base. Relief heads of Zeus
on the rim of the dish. The domed cover is decorated with sculptured
relief portraits of Zeus, Athena, and Mercury. The finial is a sculptured
floral and leaf design. **(A)**

Private Collection

16-1 Butter Dish
Tiffany & Co., Inc.
New York, New York, c. 1925
H. 4½"

Bulbous circular dish with a pierced liner. The cover slightly concave
with a conforming finial. **(C)**

16-2 Butter Dish
Ball, Black & Company
New York, New York, c. 1865
H. 6¾"

Circular dish, the bottom on four cast angular feet. Two scrolled strap
handles. The domed cover with an applied die-rolled geometrical
border and a berry finial. **(A)**

The Burt Collection

16-3 Butter Dish
Schmitz, Moore & Co.
Newark, New Jersey, c. 1920
H. 3½"

Circular pierced stand with a ball handle. Glass insert. Three ball feet. **(C)**

Author's Collection

16-4 Butter Dish
Towle Manufacturing Company
Newburyport, Massachusetts, c. 1915
D. 4"

Open, circular butter dish with a pierced strainer. Scroll and foliage edge. **(C)**

16-5 Butter Dish
Meriden Britannia Company
Meriden, Connecticut, c. 1880
D. 6⅞"

Circular dish with applied, cast splayed feet and rope handles. The domed cover bright-cut with flowers and foliage. Knife rest at the side. Silver-plated. **(C)**

Collection of Mr. & Mrs. Theodore Rockafellow
New Britain, PA

No. 4941.   No. 4993.   No. 4992.

16-6 Butter Dish (left)
Meriden Britannia Company
Meriden, Connecticut, c. 1885
H. 8" approx.

Similar in form to dishes pictured center and right, all with frames to
hold the covers when raised. Bulbous shape with a domed cover. Engraved decoration. Silver-plated. **(C)**

Butter Dish (center)
Meriden Britannia Company
Meriden, Connecticut, c. 1885
H. 8" approx.

Engraved body on four cast, splayed feet. The dome engraved with
fruit and foliage. Silver-plated. **(C)**

Butter Dish (right)
Meriden Britannia Company
Meriden, Connecticut, c. 1885
H. 7½" approx.

The circular dish on four splayed feet, the body and dome fluted. Silver-plated. **(C)**

Meriden B. catalogue, 1886
The International Silver Company Historical Library

16-7 Butter Dish
Reed & Barton
Taunton, Massachusetts, c. 1884
H. 9" approx.

Covered butter dish. Raising the handle from the horizontal to the vertical lowers the cover onto the dish. Silver-plated. **(C)**

Reed & Barton catalogue, 1884

16-8 Butter Dish
Ames Mfg. Company
Chicopee, Massachusetts, c. 1840
D. 6½"

Circular dish with two handles. The domed cover engraved, with a cow finial. Silver-plated. **(C)**

Collection of Mr. & Mrs. Theodore Rockafellow
New Britain, PA

16-9 Butter Tub
Meriden Britannia Company
Meriden, Connecticut, c. 1900
D. 6¼"

Butter dish in tub form with a
pierced insert. The dish simulates
wooden staves with metal hoops.
Silver-plated. **(C)**

Collection of Mr. & Mrs. Theodore
Rockafellow
New Britain, PA

16-10 Butter Dish (right)
Osborn Company
Lancaster, Pennsylvania, c. 1897
L. 6¾"

Butter Dish (left)
Mead & Robbins
Philadelphia, Pennsylvania, c. 1893
L. 6¾"

Identical butter dishes made by two different companies in the 1890s.
The shape reflects the new availability of butter in packaged form. The
dishes have gadrooned borders while the covers are decorated with
engraved leaf and flower designs. Both silver-plated. **(C)**

Collection of Mr. & Mrs. Theodore Rockafellow
New Britain, PA

16-11 Butter Dish
Rogers Brothers
Waterbury, Connecticut, c. 1860
D. 7½"

Butter dish with a broad beaded rim. The domed cover with a beaded
edge and a cow couchant finial. Silver-plated. **(C)**

17 | Syrup Pitchers

Syrups, such as maple, sorghum, and molasses, were used more frequently during the 19th century than they are today. The early syrup pitcher was set on a plate to catch the drips. By the 1880s a patent cut-off device inside the pitcher became a standard feature and the need for the drip plate was eliminated.

The syrup pitcher ranges from four to seven inches in height and is characterized by a close-fitting hinged lid with a thumbpiece which, when depressed, raises the lid sufficiently to allow for a steady flow. Most tea services of the period include an optional syrup pitcher in the same pattern. Porcelain syrup pitchers with silver fittings were also available.

17-O Syrup Pitcher (color plate)
Ball, Black & Company
New York, New York, 1864
H. 7½"

Tall pear-shaped pitcher on a spreading rim foot. Gadrooned border at the base. Beaded border at the rim. The sides decorated with masks and heart-shaped pendants. Domed cover and scroll handle. **(A)**

The Burt Collection

17-1 Syrup Pitcher with Waiter
Apollo Silver Co.
New York, New York, c. 1899
H. 4¼"

Pear-shaped body with broad fluting, the stepped cover with fluted edges and swirling fluted finial. Scroll handle on a circular conforming waiter. Silver-plated. **(C)**

Collection of Mr. & Mrs. Theodore Rockafellow
New Britain, PA

17-2 Syrup Pitcher
1847 Rogers Bros.
Meriden, Connecticut, c. 1900
H. 6¼"

Ovoid body with fluting at the base. Domed cover with urn-shaped finial. C-shaped handle. Silver-plated. **(C)**

Collection of Mr. & Mrs. Theodore Rockafellow
New Britain, PA

17-3 Syrup Pitcher
Meriden Britannia Company
Meriden, Connecticut, c. 1855
H. 6" approx.

Square glass pitcher with silver
mountings. Domed cover with a
woman's head finial. Harp handles and angular base. Silver-
plated. **(C)**

Meriden B. catalogue, 1855
The International Silver Company
Historical Library

17-4 Syrup Pitcher (left)
Meriden Britannia Company
Meriden, Connecticut, c. 1855
H. 7" approx.

Vase form on a spreading rim foot, the domed cover with a head finial
and thumbpiece. Angular handle. Silver-plated. **(B)**

Syrup Pitcher (right)
Meriden Britannia Company

Meriden, Connecticut, c. 1855
H. 7" approx.

Globular form with a narrow flaring neck. Domed cover with thumb-piece. Scroll handle. Silver-plated. **(B)**

Meriden B. catalogue, 1855
The International Silver Company Historical Library

17-5 Syrup Pitcher
Derby Silver Co.
Derby, Connecticut, c. 1883
H. 4¼"

Cylindrical pitcher in a carrying stand. Pitcher embossed with scenes within scrolls. C-shaped handle. Cover with thumbpiece. Silver-plated. **(B)**

Derby catalogue, 1883
The International Silver Company Historical Library

17-6 Syrup Pitcher
Derby Silver Co.
Derby, Connecticut, c. 1883
H. 5⅝"

Pear-shaped pitcher on four cast, splayed feet. The body chased with foliage. Harp handle. Cover with stepped finial and thumbpiece. Silver-plated. **(C)**

Derby catalogue, 1883
The International Silver Company Historical Library

18 | Cruet Stands

The cruet stand, or table caster, was a mainstay on dining room tables during the latter half of the 19th century and in the early part of this century. Cruet stands were mostly fashioned in silver plate and were both fanciful in form and practical in function. Their practicality lay in the realm of convenience, for the stand held virtually all the various spices and condiments needed to enliven the taste of food.

Cruet stands and pots were commonly made of glass with silver tops. The glass ranges from plain clear to cut glass in various shades of amber, blue, and red. The simplest cruet stand held two bottles, one for oil and one for vinegar (18-2); the most elaborate held six or eight containers for the various seasonings (18-3). Some later sets incorporate call bells and vases. Yet another variation is a set that revolves like a ferris wheel, with six bottles and pots making an endless round, two by two. Other caster sets revolve horizontally for easy access to all the containers (18-1).

Cruet stands are highly collectible today. The most expensively made seem to have survived the best, probably because the stands are more substantial and the accoutrements are of heavier glass. It is still rare to find a cruet stand in mint condition with all the stoppers and fittings in their original condition.

18-O Cruet Set (color plate)
Maker unknown
c. 1860
H. 10½"

Three-bottle set with claw and ball feet. Rope and tassels decorate the circular handle. The handle, edges of the waiter, and the holders embellished with a twisted rope design. Glass mustard pot with a silver lid and finial. Silver-plated. **(B)**

Private Collection

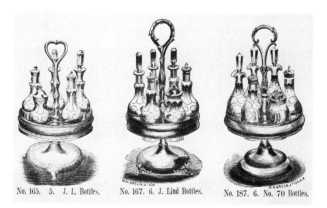

No. 165. 5. J. L. Bottles.   No. 167. 6. J. Lind Bottles.   No. 187. 6. No. 70 Bottles.

18-1 Cruet Stand (left)
Meriden Britannia Company
Meriden, Connecticut, c. 1855
H. 9" approx.

The stand holds five "Jenny Lind" bottles. Jenny Lind, the "Swedish nightingale," made her American debut in 1850. Heart-shaped handle. Flaring base ending in four splayed feet. Silver-plated. **(B)**

Cruet Stand (center)
Meriden Britannia Company
Meriden, Connecticut, c. 1855
H. 11" approx.

Six "Jenny Lind" bottles on a stand similar to the one at left, the splayed feet decorated with leaves. Silver-plated. **(B)**

Cruet Stand (right)
Meriden Britannia Company
Meriden, Connecticut, c. 1855
H. 11" approx.

Also with a six-bottle capacity; beaded edges and a stepped base. Silver-plated. **(B)**

Meriden B. catalogue, 1855
The International Silver Company Historical Library

18-2 Cruet Stand
Gorham Mfg. Company
Providence, Rhode Island
c. 1884
H. 8" approx.

Kidney-shaped two-bottle cruet stand with four splayed feet. Bottles sit in openwork frames flanking a long-legged bird. **(B)**

Gorham catalogue, 1884

18-3 Caster Set
Reed & Barton
Taunton, Massachusetts, c. 1884
H. 9½"

Caster set with six, square pressed glass bottles. Silver stand with bracket feet and a square handle. Silver-plated. **(C)**

Reed & Barton catalogue, 1884

18-4 Cruet Stand (left)
Meriden Britannia Company
Meriden, Connecticut, c. 1886
H. 9" approx.

Circular five-bottle stand on a bell-shaped pedestal. A cupid sits in a
swing between the divided handle. Silver-plated. **(B)**

Cruet Stand (right)
Meriden Britannia Company
Meriden, Connecticut, c. 1886
H. 10" approx.

Similar form with the handle decorated with foliage. Silver-plated. **(B)**

Meriden B. catalogue, 1886
The International Silver Company Historical Library

19 | Pickle Casters

Pickle casters date from the end of the 19th century when low-cost colored pressed glass became widely available. Most casters accommodate a single pickle jar, although some held two, offering variety
to the pickle connoisseur. These were the days when housewives prid-
ed themselves on the variety of pickles "put up" during the canning
season. Bread and butter pickles, mustard pickles, dill pickles, sweet
pickles, and watermelon pickles were some of the standards, and the
guest who praised a certain kind often was presented with a jar of his
own upon his departure.
   The glass pickle jar, usually round, but sometimes square, sits in a

frame with a tall handle for easy passing. Suspended on one side of the frame is a matching pickle fork to spear the juicy morsels, although an alternative pair of tongs was occasionally more appropriate for certain pickle varieties. The casters stand ten to twelve inches tall and, like the cruet stands, were sometimes left on the dining room table or sideboard so that a pickle was always available for a healthy snack.

19-O Pickle Caster (color plate)
Wilcox Silver Plate Co.
Meriden, Connecticut, c. 1890
H. 11¼"

Repoussé lid with flowers, leaves, and vines. Top of the handle decorated with dragonflies. Claw feet. Silver-plated. **(C)**

Private Collection

19-1 Pickle Caster
Barbour Silver Co.
Hartford, Connecticut, c. 1890
H. 8½"

Circular pressed glass jar in a frame with an undulate border above a spreading rim foot. Square bracket handle and pickle tongs. Silver-plated. **(C)**

Ren's Antiques
Newtown, PA

19-2 Pickle Caster
William Rogers Mfg. Co.
Hartford, Connecticut, c. 1880
H. 10"

Circular pressed glass jar in a silver stand on four openwork scroll feet. Rounded handle with a hook for pickle tongs. Engraved, domed cover with reeded finial. Silver-plated. **(C)**

Private Collection

19-3 Pickle Caster (left)
Meriden Britannia Company
Meriden, Connecticut, c. 1886
H. 9" approx.

Pickle caster on four cast splayed feet. The patented cover slides up the handle. Silver-plated. **(C)**

Pickle Caster (right)
Meriden Britannia Company
Meriden, Connecticut, c. 1886
H. 9" approx.

Pressed glass bottle with floral pattern, in a stand with four cast feet. The handle decorated with flowers and foliage. Silver-plated. **(C)**

Meriden B. catalogue, 1886
The International Silver Company Historical Library

19-4 Pickle Caster (left)
Meriden Britannia Company
Meriden, Connecticut, c. 1886
H. 8" approx.

Caster on four cast, splayed feet with stylized egg-and-dart and flower patterns. Simple round handle with a hook for pickle tongs. Silver-plated. **(C)**

Pickle Caster (right)
Meriden Britannia Company
Meriden, Connecticut, c. 1886
H. 8" approx.

Round caster on a square base, the bottle decorated with leaves and birds. The plain round handle holds an ornate pair of tongs. Silver-plated. **(C)**

Meriden B. catalogue, 1886
The International Silver Company Historical Library

19-5 Pickle Caster
Reed & Barton
Taunton, Massachusetts, c. 1884
H. 6" approx.

Round silver caster on a spreading rim foot. Domed lid with an engraved finial. Double handles, one with a holder for the pickle fork. The caster decorated with alternating bands of geometric patterns and figures of berries, leaves, and birds. Silver-plated. **(C)**

Reed & Barton catalogue, 1884

20 | Mustard Pots

The mustard pot was a necessity on the 19th-century table, but is not often used today. The mustard of the 19th century was prepared from dry mustard as it was needed and the decline of the traditional mustard pot was due, at least in part, to the production of commercial ready-to-use mustard in a conveniently sized container during the early 1900s.

During the period of its popularity, the American mustard pot was commonly manufactured in silver and silver plate. The forms usually consist of a barrel shape, a miniature mug, or a pierced silver holder for the glass insert used in all the containers. Glass liners are an obvious necessity with pierced mustard pots, and because mustard discolors silver, liners are equally advisable even if the silver containers have plain sides. The decoration and ornamentation on American pots is usually quite simple, seldom equaling the fantasies created by English silversmiths.

20-0 Mustard Pot (color plate)
Gorham Mfg. Company
Providence, Rhode Island, 1874
H. 3⅝"

Globular form on four paw feet. Fluted C-shaped handle with twisted ribbon design. Urn-shaped finial. **(B)**

The Burt Collection

20-1 Mustard Pot
Tiffany & Co., Inc.
New York, New York, c. 1925
H. 4½"

Ovoid body on a spreading rim foot. Pierced border beneath the rim. Rounded cover with finial. Glass liner. **(C)**

The Burt Collection

20-2 Mustard Pot
Gorham Mfg. Company
Providence, Rhode Island
c. 1890
H. 3½"

Concave body with scroll handle. Chased decoration of flowers, foliage, and scrolls. Domed lid with finial. **(C)**

Private Collection

20-3 Mustard Pot
Frank M. Whiting & Co.
North Attleboro, Massachusetts
c. 1900
H. 3¼"

Cylindrical, vertically pierced body with angular handle. Cover with an urn-shaped finial. Pale pink glass liner. **(C)**

Private Collection

20-4 Mustard Pot
R. Wallace & Sons Mfg. Co.
Wallingford, Connecticut
c. 1915
H. 2¾"

Cylindrical pierced body with a blue glass liner. Pierced leaf border at the rim and base. Scroll handle. Domed cover with urn-shaped finial. **(C)**

Private Collection

20-5 Mustard Pot (with pepper and open salt)
The Pairpoint Corporation
New Bedford, Massachusetts, c. 1910
H. 2"

Wire frame on ball feet, holding mustard pot and open salt-and-pepper shakers. The pepper shaker is shown removed from its holder. Silver-plated. **(C)**

Collection of Mr. & Mrs. Theodore Rockafellow
New Britain, PA

20-6 Mustard Pot (left)
Meriden Britannia Company
Meriden, Connecticut, c. 1886
H. 3"

Cylindrical pot with a hinged lid, on a spreading rim foot. Silver-plated. **(C)**

Mustard Pot (right)
Meriden Britannia Company
Meriden, Connecticut, c. 1886
H. 3"

Cylindrical pot with a hinged lid, horizontal reeded bands at top and bottom, a shaped finial, and a C-shaped handle. Silver-plated.

Meriden B. catalogue, 1886
The International Silver Company Historical Library

21 | Sugar Casters

The sugar caster, although produced by all the major silver firms during the 19th century, never achieved the popularity that it enjoyed in England. Casters with glass bodies and silver-plated or other metal tops were the most common in the late 19th century. The Colonial Revival around the beginning of the 20th century revitalized the popularity of the silver caster somewhat.

Also called a dredger or a muffineer, casters are usually five to eight inches in height, with a removable pierced top. Both granulated and powdered sugar are used in the container. Today such casters can be used for sugaring all sorts of dishes.

21-O Sugar Caster (color plate)
Tiffany & Co., Inc.
New York, New York, c. 1920
H. 7½"

Ovoid body on a swirling, fluted circular pedestal set on a square base. Chased floral decoration in quadrants below the rim. Bell-shaped cover with perforations. **(C)**

The Burt Collection

21-1 Sugar Caster
Barbour Silver Co.
Meriden, Connecticut, c. 1910
H. 4½"

Tapered cylindrical form with an overall pattern of scrolls and foliage. The perforated top continues the line of the body to a blunt tip. **(B)**

Author's Collection

21-2 Sugar Caster
Gorham Mfg. Company
Providence, Rhode Island
c. 1925
H. 7½"

Baluster-shaped body on a stepped pedestal base. Perforated cover with finial. **(C)**

I. Freeman & Son
New York, NY

21-3 Sugar Caster (left)
Gorham Mfg. Company
Providence, Rhode Island
c. 1900
H. 7½"

Tapered, hexagonal glass caster with a pierced cylindrical cover. **(C)**

Sugar Caster (right)
Gorham Mfg. Company
Providence, Rhode Island
c. 1915
H. 7½"

Vase-form body tapering to a pedestal base. Pierced bell-shaped cover with finial. **(C)**

Private Collection

21-4 Sugar Caster
Tiffany & Co., Inc.
New York, New York, c. 1900
H. 5¼"

Cylindrical body on a spreading rim foot with gadrooned edge. The lower half of the body is fluted. Flattened, dome-shaped perforated top with wrythen finial. Silver-plated. **(C)**

Collection of Mr. & Mrs. Theodore Rockafellow
New Britain, PA

21-5 Sugar Caster
Maker unknown
c. 1885
H. 4¾"

Ovoid glass body with cylindrical perforated cover. Cover decorated with leaves and vines. Silver-plated. **(D)**

Collection of Mr. & Mrs. Theodore Rockafellow
New Britain, PA

22 | Salt Cellars and Salts and Peppers

The standing salt cellar was used on banquet tables in the Middle Ages and the oft-quoted phrase "below the salt" derives from the usage of the grand or master salt cellar at the high table. Perhaps the most famous salt cellar in the world is the 16th-century gold masterpiece created by Benvenuto Cellini for Francois I of France. By the 19th century salt was commonplace on the table and relegated to a much lower place, sharing honors with pepper, mustard, etc. In the 1800s and today, salt cellars are often placed between two place settings at the table or one is found at either end of the table for passing.

Although the Reed & Barton catalogue for 1884 contained eighty-four variations of the salt cellar, their size and form varies only slightly. If footed, the cellar often has three feet (22-3), otherwise, it usually takes the form of a small shallow bowl, or occasionally an inverted cone on a short pedestal (22-4, left). Since bad luck has long been associated with the spilling of salt, salt cellars were designed so that they would not overturn easily.

Cellars are either gilt lined or have colored glass inserts (22-5), since salt standing in silver results in a chemical reaction that pits the metal. Accompanying the cellar is a salt spoon (not shown), an inch and a half to two inches long with a small round bowl.

Matching salt-and-pepper shakers were not available until the late 19th century. Shakers of the period are glass with silver or silver-plated tops (22-1), or silver-cast to resemble forms from nature, animals, and even children (22-10).

22-0 Open Salt (color plate)
Reed & Barton
Taunton, Massachusetts, c. 1880
L. 4½"

Shallow, oval blue liner in an open silver holder with four paw feet and medallions on the sides. Two loop handles. Silver-plated. **(B)**

Reed & Barton Collection

22-1 Salts and Peppers
Gorham Mfg. Company
Providence, Rhode Island, c. 1890
H. 2½"

Four matching salts and peppers with pear-shaped bodies. Scroll and flower decorations on the hips of the bodies. Rim feet. **(C)**

I. Freeman & Son
New York, NY

22-2 Salt and Pepper (left)
Gorham Mfg. Company
Providence, Rhode Island, c. 1925
H. 3½"

Cylindrical tapered bodies with domed covers and spreading rim feet. **(C)**

Salt (right)
Wood & Hughes
New York, New York, 1865
H. 5"

Vase form on a stepped pedestal base. Two scroll handles. Medallion on the side with relief head of a knight in armor. **(B)**

The Burt Collection

22-3 Open Salts
A.G. Schultz & Co.
Baltimore, Maryland, c. 1900
H. 1¹³⁄₁₆"

Pair of open salts. Bombé form with three paw feet. Repoussé flowers and foliage on a stippled ground. Clear glass liners. **(C)**

I. Freeman & Son
New York, NY

22-4 Open Salts (left)
Gorham Mfg. Company
Providence, Rhode Island, 1868
H. 1¾"

Cylindrical bowls with fluted borders on stepped pedestal bases. Gilt-lined. **(C)**

Open Salt (right)
Tuttle Silversmiths
Boston, Massachusetts, c. 1920
H. 1½"

Plain circular form with three paw feet. Blue liner. **(C)**

I. Freeman & Son
New York, NY

22-5 Open Salt
Maker unknown
Dated 1846
H. 2½"

Oval, blue glass liner in a Gothic pierced frame with four scroll feet. **(B)**

I. Freeman & Son
New York, NY

22-6 Salt and Pepper
Maker unknown
c. 1860
H. 2½"

Cylindrical, eliptically pierced holders with blue glass liners. Bulbous tops. **(B)**

I. Freeman & Son
New York, NY

22-7 Salt and Pepper
Wilcox Silver Plate Co.
Meriden, Connecticut, c. 1900
H. 2⅞"

Pear-shaped crystal bodies engraved with roses and foliage. Bulbous silver tops. **(C)**

Author's Collection

22-8 Salt and Pepper

Gorham Mfg. Company
Providence, Rhode Island, 1882
D. 1½"

Globular form with grotesque faces. The salt with yellow glass eyes, the pepper with red glass eyes. **(B)**

Private Collection

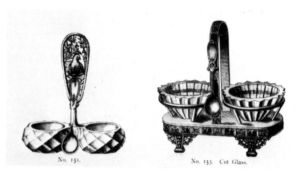

No. 151.   No. 153. Cut Glass.

22-9 Open Salts (left)
Meriden Britannia Company
Meriden, Connecticut, c. 1886
H. 3½" approx.

Double salt stand, the openwork handle with a bird and foliage design. Salt spoon clamped to the handle. Silver-plated. **(B)**

Open Salts (right)
Meriden Britannia Company
Meriden, Connecticut, c. 1886
H. 4" approx.

Silver stand with openwork frames holding two faceted glass inserts. Bail handle with salt spoon clamped to the side. The stand rests on four cast, applied openwork feet. Silver-plated. **(C)**

Meriden B. catalogue, 1886
The International Silver Company Historical Library

No. 72

22-10 Salt Shaker
Meriden Britannia Company
Meriden, Connecticut, c. 1886
H. 4" approx.

Figural salt shaker of bonneted girl with muff. The same figure is used with a napkin ring (see 26-13). Since it was common practice to exchange parts within a factory, items such as feet, finials, and handles were often available on different forms. Silver-plated. **(C)**

Meriden B. catalogue, 1886
The International Silver Company
Historical Library

23 | Compotes, Epergnes, and Centerpieces

The grand pieces used for the center of the Victorian formal table consist primarily of three forms. The basic form is the compote or comport, a shallow bowl raised on a pedestal, often with elaborate cast, applied decoration. It traditionally would be filled with fruits such as one sees in the still-life paintings of the period. The second form, the epergne, is a centerpiece that is both highly decorative and useful. It often consists of a central bowl with a number of smaller bowls on platforms surrounding the center, but can also take the form of an elaborate frame with many branches, from which hang small baskets or dishes. These containers are filled with sweetmeats, nuts, mints, or flowers.

The third and grandest form, the centerpiece, was actually the first of these forms to originate, appearing during the reign of George I in England. Its original low massive form eventually evolved into purely decorative, marginally useful centerpieces such as the Tiffany piece in 23-4, in which the shallow bowl at the top is overshadowed by the elaborate base.

23-0 Compote (color plate)
Tiffany & Company
New York, New York, c. 1860
H. 7½"

Circular bowl with cast applied border of flowers and foliage. Foliate border on the stepped pedestal base. **(B)**

The Burt Collection

23-1 Compote
Tiffany & Company
New York, New York, c. 1858
H. 6½"

Shallow circular bowl with cast, applied strawberries and vines. The base with a Greek key border with cast applied strawberries and vines above. **(A)**

The Burt Collection

23-2 Compote
Marked Ford & Tupper
c. 1860
H. 15"

Circular compote with a reeded, crenelated rim on a spreading rim foot. The pedestal decorated with cast, applied foliage and birds. The open wire handles provide perches for cast birds. The interior elaborately engraved. (Ford & Tupper may have been the retailers.) **(A)**

The Burt Collection

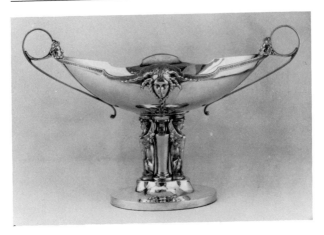

23-3 Compote
Gorham Mfg. Company
Providence, Rhode Island, c. 1865
H. 10"

Oval bowl supported by a pair of cast sphinxes back to back against a center support on an oval rim foot. Greek key border around a shaped rim. Scroll handles with cast bearded masks inside. Cast masks on the sides of the bowl. **(A)**

Lyndhurst Corporation
New York, NY

23-4 Centerpiece
Tiffany & Co., Inc.
New York, New York, c. 1872
H. 19½"

Shallow, two-handled circular bowl with a cast frieze of griffins, columns, and swags on matte ground, set on a reel-shaped pedestal. The rim foot with a border of cast putti bearing garlands. Three slender supports headed by female masks and surrounded by openwork scrolling tendrils which spread from a central vase above the triform base. **(A)**

Lyndhurst Corporation
New York, NY

23-5 Epergne
Meriden Britannia Company
Meriden, Connecticut, c. 1886
H. 19"

Circular glass bowl set in a stand formed by leaves. The whole on a slender stem with branching leaves. The base with cast leaves and swans. Silver-plated. **(B)**

Meriden B. catalogue, 1886
The International Silver Company
Historical Library

23-6 Epergne
Meriden Britannia Company
Meriden, Connecticut, c. 1886
H. 12" approx.

A sea deity, probably Poseidon, on a shell base with two sea creatures blowing shell trumpets. The central pedestal sits on a circular base bearing two glass dishes. Cast fruit and leaves surround the pedestal. Silver-plated. **(B)**

Meriden B. catalogue, 1886
The International Silver Company
Historical Library

23-7 Epergne
Meriden Britannia Company
Meriden, Connecticut, c. 1886
H. 18" approx.

Standing cupid in a shallow bowl with two maidens back to back sitting on a bulbous vase, centered in a broad shallow bowl with two shallow dishes at the sides. The whole on a trefoil base with four splayed feet. Silver-plated. **(B)**

Meriden B. catalogue, 1886
The International Silver Company
Historical Library

24 | Tazzas

The term tazza is applied to a circular shallow dish on a foot or on a stem and foot. "Tazza" is an Italian word, and in the late 16th and 17th centuries it was used to designate a wine cup with a shallow bowl. By the 18th century the term was used to designate a salver on a stemmed foot that was used to present drinks to guests. The difference between a tazza and a compote is slight, but, in general, the tazza is flat or slightly concave, while the compote is deeper and designed as a receptacle rather than a platform. The contemporary use for the tazza is primarily ornamental. It can be used as a centerpiece by itself or arranged with grapes or trailing flowers and vines.

24-0 Tazza (color plate)
Gorham Mfg. Company
Providence, Rhode Island, 1867
H. 12½"

Shallow, two-handled circular bowl with draped, classical female figures back to back against a slender support on a circular base with four Egyptian mask feet. **(A)**

The Burt Collection

24-1 Tazza
Galt & Bro.
Washington, D.C., c. 1900
H. 3¾"

Shallow circular bowl on a pedestal base with a rim foot. The edge of the bowl and the base with egg-and-dart borders enclosing a broad chased band of scrolls, bellflowers, and acanthus. **(B)**

I. Freeman & Son
New York, NY

24-2 Tazza
Brown & Spalding
1870
H. 9¾"

Shallow circular bowl with a vase-shaped support on a triangular
base. Decorative supporting scrolls attached at the middle of the support and at the base. **(B)**

I. Freeman & Son
New York, NY

24-3 Tazza
International Silver Co.
Meriden, Connecticut, c. 1920
H. 7¾"

Shallow, two-handled circular bowl on a pedestal base with a spreading rim foot. Open scroll handles. The bowl decorated with a broad border of rosettes, urns, and scrolls. **(C)**

I. Freeman & Son
New York, NY

24-4 Tazza
Dominick & Haff, Inc.
Newark, New Jersey, 1900
H. 4¼"

Shallow circular bowl with a broad reticulated rim. Pedestal foot. The rim and the foot edged with shell and gadroon border. **(B)**

I. Freeman & Son
New York, NY

24-5 Tazza
Gorham Mfg. Company
Providence, Rhode Island
c. 1865
H. 10⅛"

Oval-shaped bowl with cast monopodes flanking a cylindrical support. Greek key border at the base and along the shaped rim. **(B)**

Private Collection

24-6 Tazza
Gorham Mfg. Company
Providence, Rhode Island
c. 1870
H. 9"

Straight-sided circular bowl on a conical support and a circular rim foot. The bowl decorated with medallions and cast heads with reeded edges at the base and the rim. **(B)**

The Burt Collection

25 | Protectors and Holders

The objects in this category are designed to protect the table or the user when handling a hot platter, or to disguise a plain container. The protectors are usually trivets, while the holders were made for specific items, such as cups.

The silver-plated trivet is a form that emerged with the servantless households of the 20th century. Trivets are always plated since solid silver acts as a conductor.

In the 19th century holders were made to contain ketchup bottles, jam pots (25-6), and soft-boiled eggs (25-8). A citrus fruit holder pictured in a catalogue from the 1880s consists of a bowl with prongs inside on which the rind would be impaled. A similarly unique device was an oil lamp filler which enabled a lamp to be refilled without removing the fixture from the drawing room. The silver-plated version (25-7) is the sort of object given to someone who "had everything," and was usually fashioned from a base metal rather than silver. Silver holders for porcelain cups (25-4), individual souffle dishes (25-3), and bouillon cups are 20th century in origin.

25-0 Trivet (color plate)
R. Wallace & Sons Mfg. Co.
Wallingford, Connecticut, c. 1920
L. 6⅛"

Oval footed trivet with an openwork design of flowers and foliage. Silver-plated. **(D)**

Ren's Antiques
Newtown, PA

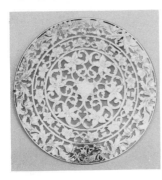

25-1 Trivet
G.K. Webster Co.
North Attleboro, Massachusetts
c. 1910
D. 7⅞"

Circular openwork trivet with three concentric circles with designs of flowers, leaves, and scrolls. Glass insert. Silver-plated. **(D)**

Ren's Antiques
Newtown, PA

25-2 Trivet
Friedman Silver Co., Inc.
Brooklyn, New York, c. 1925
D. 6⅜"

Circular openwork trivet with an engraved design. Silver-plated. **(D)**

25-3 Souffle Dishes
Maker unknown
c. 1925

L. 6″ (including handle)

Circular pierced holders with engraved handles and porcelain liners. **(D)**

Private Collection

25-4 Demitasse Holder
Maker unknown
c. 1920
H. 1¾″

Cylindrical pierced holder with a strap handle. **(D)**

Private Collection

25-5 Condiment Ring
International Silver Co.
Meriden, Connecticut, c. 1915
H. 2¼″

Cylindrical pierced ring for holding a condiment bottle. Silver-plated. **(D)**

Private Collection

25-6 Jam Jar
Meriden Britannia Company
Meriden, Connecticut, c. 1880
H. 5⅛″

Cylindrical tankard shape with a domed cover and thumbpiece. Harp handle. Cast, applied scrolls on the body. Jam jar fits inside. Silver-plated. **(C)**

Collection of Mr. & Mrs. Theodore Rockafellow
New Britain, PA

25-7 Oil Lamp Filler
Manning, Bowman & Co.
Meriden, Connecticut, c. 1880
H. 7½"

Ovoid body on a spreading rim foot. Scroll handle and long spout.
Beaded rim. Pressure pump in front of handle for filling hanging lamps.
Silver-plated. **(B)**

Collection of Mr. & Mrs. Theodore Rockafellow
New Britain, PA

25-8 Egg Cup
Maker unknown
c. 1885
H. 2½"

Egg-shaped holder with jagged
edge. Set on a heart-shaped leaf.
(D)

Author's Collection

25-9 Trivet
R. Wallace & Sons Mfg. Co.
Wallingford, Connecticut, c. 1930
L. 10¾"

Oval trivet with a deep border of entwined scrolls, flowers, and foliage.
Silver-plated. **(D)**

26 | Napkin Rings

The napkin ring in silver and silver plate enjoyed an extraordinary popularity in the United States as the country prospered during the 19th century. The ring was both a practical and aesthetic solution to the problem of clean napery before the days of the Maytag. In order that a used napkin could be returned to the same person, rings were engraved with initials or with a first name (26-2). Women and girls might use floral rings, while the males of the household might have napkin rings decorated with animals or other masculine motifs (26-8). Children began their use of napkin rings early. One might suppose that the appearance of a child at the family table would be celebrated with the gift of a napkin ring he could call his own.

The ring's rise in popularity can be charted by the number of designs available in the catalogues of the latter half of the 19th century. The Meriden Britannia catalogue of 1855 included no napkin rings; in 1861 there were seven designs; in 1867, fifteen; in 1877, thirty-nine. By 1884 the Reed & Barton catalogue offered eighty-three variants.

During the 1880s the napkin ring was seen as more than a useful appurtenance for the table and became a small piece of ornamental sculpture, the holding ring itself becoming almost subservient to the whole. Besides the figural rings so popular in the late 19th century, napkin rings at the height of their popularity combined other elements with the ring itself. Attached to the napkin holder might be an open salt-and-pepper shaker (26-12), a bud vase (26-10), a small bottle for vinegar, or a plate of butter. The practicality of these elaborations is debatable, since it would necessitate some awkward maneuvering to hold the edifice while carefully removing the napkin.

The 20th-century household, with its modern appliances and casual dining schedules (and the manufacture of disposable paper napkins), resulted in the almost total abandonment of the napkin ring by the outset of World War II. Many of the simpler narrow rings have since been cut open to make bracelets. Today napkin rings are returning to use, specifically for breakfast services or formal dinner occasions.

26-O Napkin Ring (color plate)
Maker unknown
c. 1910
H. 1⅝"

Circular, slightly concave ring with borders of scrolls, flowers, and foliage. The scrolls and flowers in blue enamel. **(C)**

Author's Collection

26-1 Napkin Ring
Reed & Barton
Taunton, Massachusetts, c. 1883
H. 3⅛"

A greyhound sejant on an oval base, bearing a napkin ring with engraved decoration. Silver-plated. **(B)**

Reed & Barton Collection

26-2 Napkin Ring (top)
Maker unknown
c. 1915
H. 1"

Child's oval ring with "DON" engraved in a scroll flanked with flowers and leaves. **(D)**

Napkin Ring (bottom left)
Maker unknown
c. 1890
H. 2"

Circular ring with beaded borders. "FRED" engraved in a parallelogram. **(D)**

Napkin Ring (bottom right)
Maker unknown
c. 1900
H. 2"

Circular ring with spiral borders. "CARRIE" in a rectangular cartouche. **(D)**

Private Collection

26-3 Napkin Ring
Maker unknown
c. 1900
H. 1½"

Octagonal bombé ring with foliate borders. **(C)**

26-4 Napkin Ring
Maker unknown
c. 1910
H. 1⅝"

Cylindrical ring with applied cast borders of scrolls and foliage. Body engraved with flowers and leaves. **(C)**

26-5 Napkin Ring
Maker unknown
c. 1890
H. 1⅝"

Initials and date between beaded borders. Flower and foliage outer borders. **(C)**

26-6 Napkin Rings
Theodore B. Starr
New York, New York, c. 1910
H. 1½"

Set of six shaped oval rings. Monogramed "MLF" surrounded by scrolls and flowers. Bellflower borders. The rings numbered 1 through 6. **(B)**

Private Collection

26-7 Napkin Ring
Tiffany & Co., Inc.
New York, New York, 1926
H. 1¼"

Child's napkin ring with an engraved design of scrolls and palmettes in panels. The center panel depicts a crouching rabbit. **(C)**

The Burt Collection

26-8 Napkin Ring
Maker unknown
c. 1885
H. 1¾"

Oval ring on four ball feet. The top is a stylized lioness's head. Engraved torsion borders. Silverplated. **(B)**

Private Collection

26-9 Napkin Ring (left)
Maker unknown
c. 1880
L. 3½"

Horse with front hoof raised, standing behind a rail fence attached to the napkin ring. Silver-plated. **(C)**

Napkin Ring (right)
Webster Mfg. Co.
Brooklyn, New York, c. 1870
L. 3⅜"

Shaped base with a rearing pony whose front legs rest against the napkin ring. Silver-plated. **(C)**

Private Collection

26-10 Napkin Ring
Meriden Britannia Company
Meriden, Connecticut, c. 1886
H. 7" approx.

Rectangular base on four circular feet with napkin ring on the left. On the right a seated cupid holds a bud vase. **(B)**

Meriden B. catalogue, 1886
The International Silver Company
Historical Library

26-11 Napkin Ring
Reed & Barton
Taunton, Massachusetts, c. 1884
H. 5½"

A peacock perched atop a chased napkin ring on a spreading foot with bellflowers pendant. Silver-plated. **(B)**

Reed & Barton catalogue, 1884

26-12 Napkin Ring (left)
Meriden Britannia Company
Meriden, Connecticut, c. 1886
H. 4" approx.

Figural napkin ring, the figure of a little girl with muff is the same as a salt shaker previously described (see 22-10). Silver-plated. **(C)**

No. 250.   No. 235.

Napkin Ring (right)
Meriden Britannia Company
Meriden, Connecticut, c. 1886
H. 3" approx.

A kitten supports a napkin ring on its back. Ring decorated with a leaf design. Silver-plated. **(C)**

Meriden B. catalogue, 1886
The International Silver Company Historical Library

26-13 Six Napkin Rings
Reed & Barton
Taunton, Massachusetts, c. 1884
H. 3" approx. (each)

Six rings with typical engraved decorations of the period—a kitten, a horse's head, a dog's head, a maple leaf, a soaring bird, and a butterfly. Silver-plated. **(C)**

Reed & Barton catalogue, 1884

27 | Toothpick and Spoon Holders

Some form of the toothpick has probably been in use since man first began to eat meat, but it was the industrial revolution in the 19th century that resulted in the modern toothpick, the shape of which has changed little in the last 100 years. A holder designed for toothpicks was first patented in 1875, but enjoyed a relatively brief popularity. By the 1880s, etiquette books deplored the use of the toothpick in public, and, although the holder has remained on the family table right up to the present day, it was banned from the formal table by 1910. The holder's size makes it a manageable form to collect today, although it has little practical use.

Spoon holders were left on the family table during the 19th century so that a clean spoon was readily available. Teaspoons were used for so many different purposes during the meal that, rather than placing them in a table setting, they were made available as they were needed. The spoon holder was also offered as an extra for the tea service during the 1870s and '80s. The most elaborate form available was the sugar bowl, with the spoon rack surrounding it (27-3). The spoon holder in its simplest form resembles a deep sugar bowl without a cover (27-2). It is sometimes difficult to distinguish between a sugar bowl and a spoon holder, although a look inside will often reveal the marks made by the spoons over the years.

27-O Toothpick Holder (color plate, left)
Derby Silver Co.
Derby, Connecticut, c. 1890
H. 2"

Pear-shaped, with engraved design of waves at the bottom. Silver-plated. **(C)**

Spoon Holder (color plate, right)
Maker unknown
c. 1890
H. 5⅞"

Vase-form spoon holder on a bell-shaped pedestal. Engraved upper body. Cornucopia handles. Silver-plated. **(C)**

Collection of Mr. & Mrs. Theodore Rockafellow
New Britain, PA

27-1 Spoon Holder
Ball, Black & Company
New York, New York, 1865
H. 11½"

Circular spoon rack for twelve spoons on a slender central support surmounted by a crossbar with a medallion in the middle. The whole on a stepped base. **(B)**

The Burt Collection

27-2 Spoon Holder
Simpson, Hall, Miller & Co.
Wallingford, Connecticut
c. 1870
H. 5¾"

Urn-shaped body on a pedestal base. Two scroll handles. The body engraved with stylized flowers. Silver-plated. **(B)**

Private Collection

27-3 Spoon Holder
Forbes Silver Co.
Meriden, Connecticut, c. 1895
H. 5"

Combination spoon holder and sugar bowl. Rack for spoons just below the rim. Two scroll handles. The domed cover topped by a barley-head finial. **(B)**

Private Collection

No. 3126. Spoon Holder.

27-4 Spoon Holder
Derby Silver Co.
Derby, Connecticut, c. 1883
H. 5¼"

Ovoid, stylized flower container on an undulating stem. A cast figure of a fairy with a watering pot is poised over the holder. Lily-pad-shaped base. Silver-plated. **(B)**

Derby catalogue, 1883
The International Silver Company
Historical Library

27-5 Spoon Holder
Derby Silver Co.
Derby, Connecticut, c. 1883
H. 4"

Loving cup with harp handles on a bell-shaped base. Row of fluting where the bottoms of the handles join the body. Silver-plated. **(C)**

Derby catalogue, 1883
The International Silver Company
Historical Library

27-6 Toothpick Holder
Derby Silver Co.
Derby, Connecticut, c. 1888
H. 3"

Toothpick holder in the form of a barrel on a stepped pedestal base. A male figure with cap doffed and arm raised holds a simulated rope attached to the "barrel." Chased and gilt-lined. **(C)**

27-7 Toothpick Holder
Derby Silver Co.
Derby, Connecticut, c. 1888
H. 3"

The identical barrel form rests on a one-wheeled cart, its handles held by a small boy. Chased and gilt-lined. **(C)**

28 | Knife Rests

The knife rest was a necessary adjunct to the carving set. Nineteenth-century novels abound with descriptions of the Sunday dinner as father stood at the head of the table and carved as carefully and precisely as a surgeon. After each diner had his choice of meat, the carving knife was placed on the rest until additional portions were requested. Knife rests are simple, highly utilitarian devices designed to protect the table cloth from dripping grease. They consist of twin mounts with a two to four-inch bar in-between on which the knife rests. Decorations of scrolls or animals at the end are almost always symmetrical. Smaller knife rests were made for use at individual place settings. Today these are quite rare.

28-O Knife Rest (color plate)
Unger Bros.
Newark, New Jersey, c. 1900
L. 3¼"

A simple dumbbell form without ornamentation. This was also a common form in cut crystal. **(C)**

Collection of The Newark Museum
Newark, NJ

28-1 Pair of Knife Rests
Maker unknown
c. 1900
L. 3"

Triangular scroll supports with twisted rope forms for rests. **(C)**

Private Collection

No. 32.

28-2 Knife Rest
Meriden Britannia Company
Meriden, Connecticut, c. 1886
L. 2"

Knife rest, the supporting members consist of three-dimensional figures of two crawling boys. Silver-plated. **(B)**

Meriden B. catalogue, 1886
The International Silver Company
Historical Library

155

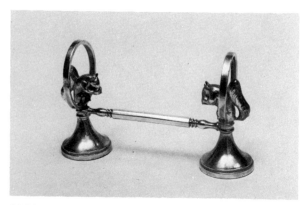

28-3 Knife Rest
Benjamin Mayo
Newark, New Jersey, c. 1885
L. 4½"

Supports of squirrels in ring perches facing each other. Silver-plated.
(B)

Private Collection

28-4 Knife Rest
Derby Silver Co.
Derby, Connecticut, c. 1883
H. 2¼"

Winged male figure with musical instrument on a pedestal. The knife rest supported at the other end by a shell ornament. Silver-plated. **(B)**

Derby catalogue, 1883
The International Silver Company
Historical Library

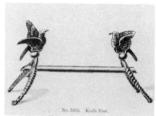

28-5 Knife Rest
Derby Silver Co.
Derby, Connecticut, c. 1883
H. 1½"

Birds with spread wings on twisted wishbone-form supports. Silver-plated. **(B)**

Derby catalogue, 1883
The International Silver Company
Historical Library

29 | Bells

A table bell was used in the 19th century as a means to summon a ser-
vant to serve a course, remove plates, or bring tea. There are three
necessary parts to the traditional form: the resonant cup, the clapper
suspended in the interior of the cup, and the handle. The former two
parts are always of metal; the cup of an alloy, sometimes silver, and
the clapper of iron. The handle may be of the same material as the
cup, or it may be made of wood, ivory, etc. Its form is usually that of a
long extended knob or hoop (29-1). A variant is the handbell in the
form of a lady, in which case the wide skirt of the dress forms the cup,
while the upper torso serves as the handle.

In the late 19th century another form of bell was manufactured in
which the sound is caused by pressure on a knob which is activated
by means of a spring (29-4). These bells were used commercially on
hotel reception desks to summon bellboys or on a teacher's desk to
arouse the attention of a class. The cup can be concave or convex.

29-0 Bell (color plate)
Howard & Co.
New York, New York, 1888
H. 4 ⅛ "

Ovoid cup with repoussé scrolls and flowers. Long, slim, tapered handle with an urn-shaped finial. **(B)**

Ren's Antiques
Newtown, PA

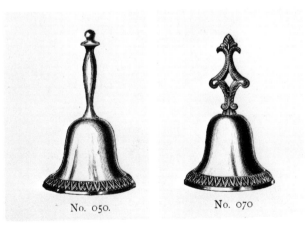

No. 050.　　No. 070

29-1 Bell (left)
Meriden Britannia Company

Meriden, Connecticut, c. 1861
H. 3½" approx.

Flared cup with engraved border and slender vase-form handle with finial. Silver-plated. **(C)**

Bell (right)
Meriden Britannia Company
Meriden, Connecticut, c. 1861
H. 3¾" approx.

Identical cup with an open handle and trefoil finial. Silver-plated. **(C)**

Meriden B. catalogue, 1886
The International Silver Company Historical Library

29-2 Bell
Gorham Mfg. Company
Providence, Rhode Island, 1884
H. 3⅜"

Flared cup with single interlaced band between two bands of beading. Baluster handle. **(C)**

Ren's Antiques
Newtown, PA

No. 023.

No. 025.

29-3 Bell (left)
Meriden Britannia Company
Meriden, Connecticut, c. 1886
H. 3½" approx.

Flared, slightly convex cup with vase-form handle. Band of reeding and ball finial. Silver-plated. **(C)**

Bell (right)
Meriden Britannia Company
Meriden, Connecticut, c. 1886
H. 3¾" approx.

Convex cup, the lower portion engraved. Vase-form handle. Silver-plated. **(C)**

Meriden B. catalogue, 1886
The International Silver Company
Historical Library

29-4 Bell
Meriden Britannia Company
Meriden, Connecticut, c. 1886
H. 5½" approx.

Push bell on a stem, grasped by a hand mounted on a spreading rim base. Silver-plated. **(C)**

Meriden B. catalogue, 1886
The International Silver Company
Historical Library

30 | Wine and Liquor Accessories

Silver is more commonly used for drinking accessories than for the cups and goblets themselves. Double-wall ice buckets, ice tongs, wine coolers, cocktail shakers, flasks, and other larger pieces are found most often in silver plate. Smaller items, such as bottle openers, jiggers, and funnels, are usually sterling, often in combination with stainless steel.

There was, indeed, a proliferation of drinking accoutrements in the 19th century. The 1898 Gorham catalogue listed ale mugs; bitters bottles; bottle holders for ginger ale, soda, and wine; bottle stands; funnels; glass holders; hot whiskey pitchers; ice bowls; ice picks; ice pitchers; ice scoops; liquor labels; nutmeg graters; punch bowls; shakers; spice stands; strainers; tumblers; urns; and wine coolers. All these forms are functional and can be used for the same purposes today.

30-0 Cocktail Shaker and Goblets (color plate)
The Weidlich Bros. Mfg. Co.
Bridgeport, Connecticut, c. 1920
D. 13⅜" (tray); H. 9⅛" (shaker); H. 4⅜" (goblets)

Tapering cylindrical cocktail shaker with elaborate engravings. Short covered spout, harp handle, and bail handle. Four matching cocktail goblets on a similarly decorated waiter. "Tapestry" pattern. Silver-plated. **(C)**

Collection of Mr. & Mrs. Theodore Rockafellow
New Britain, PA

30-1 Wine Cooler
Gorham & Company
Providence, Rhode Island
c. 1865
H. 6"

Urn-shaped wine cooler with engraved and repoussé flowers and foliage. Two grotesque animal heads with rings in their mouths form the handles. **(B)**

The Burt Collection

30-2 Cocktail Shaker
Homan Manufacturing Company
Cincinnati, Ohio, c. 1925
H. 9⅞"

Vase-shaped cocktail shaker on a spreading rim foot. Covered spout and angular handle. Silver-plated. **(C)**

30-3 Ice Bucket
Fisher Silversmiths
Jersey City, New Jersey, c. 1935
H. 12"

Ovoid body on a thick, flared pedestal. Flat cover with a conforming finial. Silver-plated. **(D)**

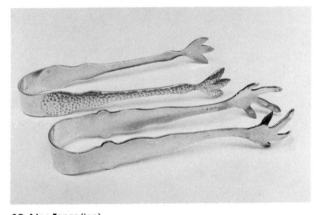

30-4 Ice Tongs (top)
Apollo Silver Co.
New York, New York, 1915
L. 6⅞"

Ice Tongs (bottom)
Paye & Baker Mfg. Co.
North Attleboro, Massachusetts, c. 1910
L. 6"

Two similar pairs of ice tongs, each with hammered surface, the top with a stippled effect. Both silver-plated. **(D)**

Collection of Mr. & Mrs. Theodore Rockafellow
New Britain, PA

30-5 Jigger
Tiffany & Co., Inc.
New York, New York, 1938
H. 2⅛"

Flared cup with simple loop handle. Reeded band at the base. **(C)**

Author's Collection

30-6 Jigger
Wm. E. Hunt Co.
Providence, Rhode Island
c. 1930
H. 3¾"

Reversible double and single jigger separated by a scrolled band. **(C)**

30-7 Funnel
Maker unknown
c. 1880
L. 3¼"

Wine funnel with serrated edge and ring handle. Silver-plated. **(C)**

Collection of Mr. & Mrs. Theodore Rockafellow
New Britain, PA

30-8 Flask
Maker unknown
c. 1910
H. 8½"

Oblong glass bottle with a silver base and top. **(C)**

I. Freeman & Son
New York, NY

30-9 Flask (left)
Meriden Britannia Company
Meriden, Connecticut, c. 1886
H. 6" approx.

Oblong flask with a broad band of engraved leaves and flowers. Silver-plated. **(C)**

Flask (right)
Meriden Britannia Company
Meriden, Connecticut, c. 1886
H. 6" approx.

Flat ovoid body with an engraved design of stems and flowers. Silver-plated. **(C)**

Meriden B. catalogue, 1886
The International Silver Company Historical Library

II THE DRAWING ROOM TABLE

31 | Tea and Coffee Services

Tea drinking in the 19th century was almost as popular in the United States as it was in England. Before 1850, tea and coffeepots were available in sterling, but most often were made of pottery or porcelain, the most desirable of which were the Chinese export services. The advent of Britannia ware and silver plate relegated porcelain to the attic, since metalware was far more serviceable than china.

The basic tea and coffee service consists of a coffeepot, a teapot, a sugar bowl, a cream pitcher, and a waste bowl. Additional pieces include a hot water jug, a tea kettle, a spoon holder, a syrup pitcher, a milk jug, and a butter dish. The breakfast set (31-6, 31-7), also called a cabaret set or a tête-è-tête set, consisted of a small coffeepot and a sugar bowl and creamer to be used for two people.

Most tea and coffee services made during the 1850s and '60s are characterized by high pedestal bases, the tea and coffeepots often holding two or three quarts. Handles were first made of wood, ivory, or mother-of-pearl. Decoration in the 1850s was either plain or embossed, but by the 1860s bright-cut and engraved decorations were cut into the surface.

The 1870s saw pots raised on four feet. Toward the end of the decade the influence of Charles Eastlake's designs became apparent following the American publication of his **Hints on Household Taste** in 1872. The angularity and sparseness of Eastlake's designs were his answer to the rococo.

The 1880s witnessed a return to footless pots, but without the high pedestal. Again, there was a great deal of chasing, and, by the 1890s, embossed designs returned to popularity. There were literally hundreds of designs in silver and silver plate. Some retained their popularity and remained in stock for twenty or thirty years, although certain designs and forms are representative of a particular decade. The Colonial Revival saw a return to the adaptations of 18th- and early-19th-century designs, but the extravagant service in silver plate was no longer available by 1910.

31-O Tea and Coffee Service (color plate)
Wm. Adams
New York, New York, c. 1840
H. 15½" (water pitcher); H. 13½" (coffee pot); H. 12½" (teapot);
    H. 9½" (creamer); H. 10½" (sugar); H. 8" (hot milk pitcher);
    H. 5½" (waste bowl)

Pear-shaped bodies with repoussé decoration of flowers and foliage. Rustic scroll handles with grapes and vine decoration. Finials of grapes and stems. Pedestal bases shaped with repoussé decoration. **(A)**

The Burt Collection

31-1 Tea Service
Jones, Ball & Poor
Boston, Massachusetts, c. 1846
H. 8½" (teapot); H. 7¼" (creamer); H. 8" (sugar); H. 4½" (waste bowl)

Pear-shaped lobed bodies on spreading rim feet. The bodies with repoussé flowers and foliage. Finials of American Indian figures performing ethnic tasks. **(A)**

The Burt Collection

31-2 Tea and Coffee Service
Gorham Mfg. Company
Providence, Rhode Island, c. 1888

H. 12½" (kettle); H. 7½" (coffeepot); H. 5½" (teapot); H. 4½" (sugar); H. 2¾" (creamer); H. 2¼" (waste bowl)

Six-piece tea and coffee service with fluted bottoms and repoussé floral tops and covers. **(B)**

Gorham catalogue, 1888

31-3 Tea Service
Tiffany & Co., Inc.
New York, New York, c. 1906
H. 5½" (teapot); H. 3½" (cream and sugar)

Bulbous bodies with fluting where the ball feet join the body. Angular handles on sugar bowl and creamer. Angular wooden handles on the teapot. Made in England for Tiffany. **(B)**

The Burt Collection

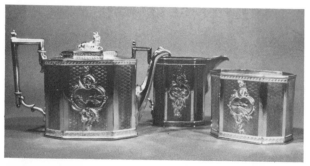

31-4 Tea Service
Reed & Barton
Taunton, Massachusetts, c. 1858
H. 6³⁄₁₆" (teapot); H. 3⅞" (sugar); H. 3½" (creamer)

Octagonal straight-sided teapot, sugar bowl, and creamer. The teapot with a sphinx-like figure on the lid, all with Greek key bands at the top and bottom. Silver-plated. **(B)**

Reed & Barton Collection

31-5 Breakfast Set
Wm. B. Kerr & Co.
Newark, New Jersey, c. 1900
H. 8¾" (pot); H. 4⅛" (creamer); H. 3⅝" (sugar); L. 10⅛" (tray)

Pear-shaped bodies, the coffeepot with an elongated neck and a long slender spout. Repoussé with a design of poppies and foliage. Matching oval waiter. **(B)**

Collection of The Newark Museum
Newark, NJ

31-6 Breakfast Set
Unger Bros.
Newark, New Jersey, c. 1900
H. 9½" (pot); H. 3¼" (creamer); H. 2¼" (sugar); L. 14" (waiter)

Similar in shape to the Kerr set (see 31-5), with slightly more bulbous bodies. The pot, sugar, and creamer chased and repoussé with flowers and foliage. Matching waiter. **(B)**

31-7 Tea and Coffee Service
Meriden Britannia Company
Meriden, Connecticut, c. 1886
H. 12" approx. (urn); L. 28" approx. (tray)

Seven-piece tea and coffee service on a conforming tray. Ovoid

bodies embossed with flowers and foliage on spreading rim feet. Silver-plated. **(C)**

Meriden B. catalogue, 1886
The International Silver Company Historical Library

31-8 Coffeepot with Cream and Sugar

Goodnow & Jenks
Boston, Massachusetts, c. 1900
H. 9½" (coffeepot); 3½" (cream and sugar)

Tall ovoid coffeepot with fluting from top to bottom. The matching creamer and sugar bowl are similar but more compressed. **(C)**

I. Freeman & Son
New York, NY

31-9 Tea and Coffee Service
Reed & Barton
Taunton, Massachusetts, c. 1860
H. 11½" (pots); H. 6⅜" (pitcher); H. 10¼" (sugar)

Urn-shaped bodies with stepped pedestal bases and stepped lids. Beading around bases and rims. The coffeepot, sugar bowl, and creamer decorated with crests surrounding initials. The teapot with identical shape and finial, the body decorated with wreaths. Silver-plated. **(C)**

Collection of Mr. & Mrs. Theodore Rockafellow
New Britain, PA

31-10 Tea and Coffee Service
Gorham Mfg. Company
Providence, Rhode Island, 1881
H. 6" (coffeepot); H. 4½" (teapot); H. 6½" (sugar); H. 2½" (creamer);
H. 2⅝" (waste bowl)

Asymmetrical Anglo-Japanese floral decoration within hammered and crackled surround in repoussé around the circular bodies of each piece. Cast anthemia and floral border around square rims. Gadrooned handles and spouts. Square lids similarly decorated, with cast pineapple finials. **(B)**

32 | Teapots

The silver teapot, used in conjunction with fine china, stands out and presents an even more attractive sight than a complete silver service. It certainly is more appropriate for a family tea or for tea with one or two guests. Indeed, purchase of a teapot alone was more comon than acquisition of a whole service. Although Reed & Barton's catalogue for 1884 lists six teapots and eighty-one tea services, it must be realized that all the pieces in the tea service could be bought separately, and often the teapot was the first item purchased. Additional pieces could be added in the same pattern over the years.

32-O Teapot (color plate)
Gorham & Company
Providence, Rhode Island, c. 1865
H. 6½"

Cylindrical body on a spreading rim foot. Cast, applied medallions on the sides. The angular handle and the spout decorated with ribbons and bows. The ribbon on the spout supports a large medallion. **(B)**

The Burt Collection

32-1 Teapot

Bailey & Company
Philadelphia, Pennsylvania
c. 1848
H. 10½"

Vase-shaped body on a pedestal foot. Scroll-shaped spout and ser-
pent handle with two heads and two tails. Bright-cut cartouches on
either side, one enclosing armorials, the other a monogram. Bright-
cut borders. The domed cover with an urn-shaped finial. Designed by George B. Sharp for Bailey. **(A)**

Lyndhurst Corporation
New York, NY

32-2 Teapot
Lincoln & Foss
Boston, Massachusetts, c. 1850
H. 10½"

Inverted pear-shaped body on a stepped circular pedestal with a rim
foot. Beaded borders at the lip, shoulder, and base of the body, the
rim foot with an undulate border. The body decorated with repoussé
rococo flowers, foliage, and scrolls. Scroll-shaped spout and handle,
the shaped cover with a cast bud finial. Made of coin silver, but typical
of the forms produced in sterling and silver plate. **(A)**

Lyndhurst Corporation
New York, NY

32-3 Teapot
Tiffany & Co., Inc.
New York, New York, 1900
H. 8¾"

Shield-shaped oval body tapering to a spreading pedestal with a rim
foot. Scroll-shaped spout and angular handle. Domed cover with an
urn-shaped finial. The whole decorated in the neoclassical style with
medallions and swags within fluted panels. **(C)**

I. Freeman & Son
New York, NY

32-4 Teapot
Towle Silversmiths
Newburyport, Massachusetts
c. 1915
H. 4" approx.

Squat bulbous form on a reeded
foot. Short spout and C-shaped
handle forking at both ends. The
domed cover with a conforming
finial. **(C)**

Towle catalogue, c. 1915

32-5 Teapot
Wilcox Silver Plate Co.
Meriden, Connecticut, c. 1887
H. 7½"

Pear-shaped body with swirling flutes on the lower half. Scroll-shaped spout and C-shaped handle. The cover decorated with swirling flutes and a ball finial. Silver-plated. **(C)**

Collection of Mr. & Mrs. Theodore Rockafellow
New Britain, PA

33 | Coffeepots and Urns

In the United States coffee gradually replaced tea as the national drink during the 19th and early 20th centuries. The popularity of after-dinner coffee resulted in the manufacture of coffeepots that were simply larger versions of the teapot. In fact, when the silver coffeepot was first designed as a single item, its form echoed the porcelain of the 18th century (the lighthouse coffeepot was first available in Chinese export porcelain). The problem of silver as a conductor of heat, however, necessitated coffeepot handles made of wood (33-5), ivory (33-0), or other materials.

The coffee urn was used when large amounts of coffee were to be consumed. The beverage was brewed separately and poured into the urn, which usually included a heating device beneath. Coffee urns were larger than tea urns, which were used for hot water to be added to already steeped tea.

33-O Coffeepot (color plate)
Barbour Silver Co.
Meriden, Connecticut, c. 1920
H. 7"

Vase-shaped body on a spreading rim foot. Scroll-shaped spout with simulated ivory handle at right angles to the spout. Shaped, hinged dome cover with an ovoid, simulated ivory finial. **(C)**

Author's Collection

33-1 Coffee Urn

Reed & Barton
Taunton, Massachusetts, c. 1850
H. 18"

Cylindrical tapered urn flared at the base. Spigot with ivory handle at base with applied scroll decoration where the spigot is attached and at the shoulders where the handles are attached. The body fluted, with the fluting continuing onto the cover. Cover with a floral finial. The whole on an openwork circular base with four splayed feet. Silver-plated. **(B)**

Reed & Barton Collection

33-2 Coffee Urn
Gebelein Silversmiths
Boston, Massachusetts, c. 1910
H. 18½"

Urn form on a square base with four claw-and-ball feet. Reeded, looped strap handles. Spool-shaped cover with pineapple finial. Faceted sides engraved with ribbon-tied floral swags bearing an oval open medallion. Spigot with an ivory handle. **(B)**

Lyndhurst Corporation
New York, NY

33-3 Coffeepot
Kidney, Cann & Johnson
New York, New York, c. 1850
H. 11"

Pear-shaped body on a spreading rim foot. Scroll-shaped spout and

harp handle. Cast, applied medallion on the side. Cover with a bud finial. **(A)**

The Burt Collection

33-4 Coffeepot
Ball, Black & Company
New York, New York, c. 1855
H. 10"

Lobed, pear-shaped body embossed and chased with a basket weave design with a matte finish. Cornucopia handle and spout. Oval cartouches set in double-trefoil banding at borders, around handle, and around neck. Large cartouches on both sides of the body. Designed by Edgar M. Eoff and George L. Sheppard for Ball, Black & Company. **(A)**

Lyndhurst Corporation
New York, NY

33-5 Coffeepot
Baldwin & Miller, Inc.
Newark, New Jersey, c. 1925
H. 10½"

Cylindrical pot, tapered to a reeded base. Scroll-shaped spout and double-C-scroll wooden handle. Hinged dome cover with a reeded finial. **(C)**

The Burt Collection

33-6 Coffeepot
Tiffany & Co., Inc.
New York, New York, c. 1920
H. 9½"

Oval tapered body on a pedestal with a reeded rim foot. Scroll-shaped spout and angular handle. Bell-shaped cover with a baluster finial. **(C)**

33-7 Coffeepot
F.B. Rogers Silver Co.
Taunton, Massachusetts, c. 1940
H. 9¼"

Ovoid body with a scroll-shaped spout and straight wooden handle at right angles to the spout. Hinged dome cover with an inverted urn-shaped finial. **(C)**

33-8 Coffee Urn

John Carrow
Philadelphia, Pennsylvania
c. 1885
H. 16"

Two-handled, vase-shaped urn on a tall openwork stand. The globular section engraved with flowers and foliage. Spigot with an ivory handle. Stepped, dome cover with a fan-shaped finial. Silver-plated. **(B)**

Private Collection

No. 1931 URN.

33-9 Coffee Urn
Meriden Britannia Company
Meriden, Connecticut, c. 1886
H. 16" approx.

Cylindrical urn on an open stand with four splayed legs. Engraved wide border where the lower end of the handles meet the body. A narrow engraved band below the spigot. Stepped cover with a fan-shaped finial. Silver-plated. **(B)**

Meriden B. catalogue, 1886
The International Silver Company
Historical Library

34 | Teakettles

Teakettles were an extravagance, even in silver plate, for all but the grandest households. A hot water jug was more commonly found with a tea service tnan a kettle on a stand. The teakettle required a spirit lamp which gave off heat that was undesirable at any time other than in cold weather. Only a few of the tea services catalogued in the 19th century offered kettles as part of the service. Undoubtedly, they could be purchased through special order, but the cost and their impracticality made them scarce. Today, with less household help available, a kettle is more practical. A tea service complete with a kettle enables the hostess to set up for teatime without having to leave her guests to refill a hot water pot.

34-O Tilting Teakettle (color plate)
Wilcox Silver Plate Co.
Meriden, Connecticut, c. 1910
H. 13¼"

Shield-shaped body with projections on either side that fit into the stand, holding the kettle above the heat and enabling it to tilt. Stand with hexagonal base. Scroll-shaped spout, stepped hinged cover with finial, and arched bail handle. Silver-plated. **(C)**

Collection of Mr. & Mrs. Theodore Rockafellow
New Britain, PA

34-1 Teakettle
Howard & Co.

New York, New York, 1909
H. 13½"

Lobed, globular-shaped body with scroll-shaped spout and arched
bail handle connected to the body with double C-scrolls. Conforming
cover with a lobed finial. Circular openwork stand on three S-scrolled
and splayed legs. **(C)**

I. Freeman & Son
New York, NY

34-2 Teakettle
Towle Silversmiths
Newburyport, Massachusetts
c. 1915
H. 12" approx.

Oval, shield-shaped teakettle.
The cover, shoulder, and lower
part of the body are fluted. The
stand with scrolled rests for the
double supports on either side.
The base of the stand and the feet
are also fluted. **(C)**

Towle catalogue, c. 1915

34-3 Teakettle
Towle Silversmiths
Newburyport, Massachusetts
c. 1915
H. 13" approx.

Teakettle on a stand with scrolled
rests for the double supports on
either side. Fleur-de-lis between
the scrolls. The ovoid-shaped kettle with a domed lid and floral
finial. Scrolled spout and double-
scroll fixed handle. The lid with a
floral border matching the borders on the base of the teakettle
and the stand. **(C)**

Towle catalogue, c. 1915

34-4 Teakettle
Gorham Mfg. Company
Providence, Rhode Island, c. 1888
H. 12½"

Kettle with a bulbous body, domed lid, and bud finial. Mounted on a stand with four splayed feet. The whole chased and repoussé with flowers and foliage. **(C)**

---

35 | Sugar Bowls and Cream Pitchers

Sugar bowls and cream pitchers were the most popular 19th-century tablewares. Both forms were introduced as part of elaborate tea services during the 18th century. In the latter half of the 19th century silver and silver-plated bowl-and-pitcher sets might be the only silver objects on the modest dining room table.

Victorian silver sugar bowls and pitchers were more utilitarian in form than those of the previous century. Handles are an integral part of their design, facilitating passing from one person to another. The shapes are also essentially utilitarian. Squat and bulbous with a low center of gravity to preclude spillage, their beauty lies in the decoration. Applied figures, bright cutting, and engraving were the principal techniques employed; the decoration usually consisting of flora and fauna motifs, although classical motifs are also common (35-5). Repoussé was rarely employed since this made the task of washing more difficult.

By the mid-19th century, sugar had become relatively cheap and the sugar bowl acquired a permanent place on the table, easily available whenever coffee, tea, or cold drinks were served. Bowls of the Victorian period, unlike their 18th-century predecessors, seldom have lids unless they are part of a larger service. The matching cream pitchers echo the utilitarian shapes of the sugar bowls (35-4). The footed pitcher accompanies the tea service and was used only by the server and not passed around the table.

An interesting later form designed to accommodate cube or loaf sugar, is the domino sugar holder, a V-shaped pierced rack available in sterling or silver plate (35-7). Although fairly common, its use is sometimes a mystery to dealers and owners.

35-O Sugar and Creamer (color plate)
Bailey & Company
Philadelphia, Pennsylvania, c. 1846
H. 8" (sugar); H. 7½" (creamer)

Pitcher with a helmet top on a short neck above an ovoid body with engraved swags. Sugar bowl with an ovoid body and slightly domed cover with an urn-shaped finial. Both pieces with twisted, rope-like scroll handles and stepped bases. **(A)**

The Burt Collection

35-1 Sugar and Creamer
Gorham Mfg. Company
Providence, Rhode Island, c. 1890
H. 3½" (sugar); H. 5¾" (creamer)

Oval open sugar with applied cast handles. Pear-shaped pitcher with a scroll handle. Both on scroll feet. The bodies repoussé with rococo decoration. Gilt-lined. **(B)**

I. Freeman & Son
New York, NY

35-2 Sugar and Creamer
International Silver Co.

Meriden, Connecticut, c. 1915
H. 7½" (sugar); H. 5½" (creamer)

Ovoid bodies on flared pedestal feet. Scroll handles and engraved pendant foliage and bellflower decoration. Sugar with a bell-shaped lid and artichoke finial. **(C)**

I. Freeman & Son
New York, NY

35-3 Sugar and Creamer
Jacobi & Jenkins
Baltimore, Maryland, c. 1895
H. 7" (sugar); H. 5¼" (creamer)

Ovoid bodies with pierced galleries. Four cast, applied paw feet with acanthus leaves joined to the body. Scroll handles. Pineapple finial on domed lid. **(B)**

I. Freeman & Son
New York, NY

35-4 Sugar and Creamer

Gorham Mfg. Company
Providence, Rhode Island, c. 1880
H. 6" (sugar); H. 4¾" (creamer)

Pear-shaped bodies on spreading rim feet. Gadrooned lip and double-scroll handles. The domed cover with a lobed finial. **(B)**

I. Freeman & Son
New York, NY

35-5 Sugar Bowl
Ball, Black & Company
New York, New York, 1868
L. 10½"

Circular covered sugar bowl on a spreading rim foot. The body decorated with beading and a Greek key border. The cast handles attached at the bottom with masks. **(A)**

The Burt Collection

35-6 Sugar Basket
Gorham Mfg. Company
Providence, Rhode Island, 1910
H. 5½"

Openwork basket with a pierced bail handle and a spreading rim foot. **(C)**

Private Collection

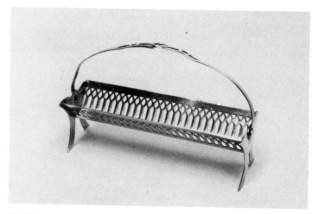

35-7 Sugar Cube Holder
Maker unknown
c. 1920
L. 4"

V-shaped container for lump sugar. Openwork sides and an openwork bail handle. **(D)**

Author's Collection

35-8 Creamer
Gorham Mfg. Company
Providence, Rhode Island, c. 1920
H. 2¾"

Bulbous body on a rim foot. Gadrooned border below the rim. Applied, cast scroll handle. **(C)**

35-9 Creamer on Sugar Tray
Unger Bros.
Newark, New Jersey, c. 1900
H. 5½"

Baluster-form pitcher with a shaped lip. Scroll handle. Pitcher fits into a raised stand in the center of the sugar tray. The sugar tray with an openwork bail handle. **(B)**

Collection of The Newark Museum Newark, NJ

35-10 Sugar Bowl
Simpson, Hall, Miller & Co.
Wallingford, Connecticut
c. 1875
H. 8½"

Vase-shaped body with a domed cover. Four applied, cast feet with a floral design. Complementary scroll handles and finial. The loop handles applied at the lower end only. Silver-plated. **(C)**

Private Collection

35-11 Sugar and Creamer
Maker unknown
c. 1910
H. 2½" (creamer); H. 2⅛" (sugar); L. 9¼" (tray)

Stylized Art Nouveau repoussé design of flowers and vines, on a shaped tray decorated similarly. Silver-plated. **(C)**

Private Collection

35-12 Cream Pitcher
Whiting Mfg. Co.
Bridgeport, Connecticut, c. 1914
H. 5"

A helmet top on a hexagonal lower half decorated with beading and foliate swags. Cast scroll handle. Hexagonal pedestal base. **(C)**

35-13 Teapot and Creamer
Apollo Silver Co.
New York, New York, 1912
H. 4½"

Two-sectioned teapot and creamer. Cylindrical creamer with an inset lid that fits the teapot also. The teapot is a tapered cylindrical form with scroll handles wrapped with rattan. Reeded borders on both pieces. Silver-plated. **(D)**

35-14 Cream Pitcher
Reed & Barton
Taunton, Massachusetts, c. 1875
H. 5⅛"

Helmet-shaped cream pitcher with a ruby red insert, the body pierced with a design of crescents and circular perforations in a diamond shape, on a stepped pedestal base. Silver-plated. **(B)**

36 | Tea Accessories

Tea in the 19th century came in loose form; its use made caddies, caddy spoons, and strainers a necessity. A tea caddy with two compartments, such as the one illustrated in 36-1, made it possible for the tea brewer to mix two kinds of tea, creating a unique blend. As more varieties of mixed blends became available, a single compartment sufficed.

Tea caddy spoons are highly collectible and have been made in a great variety of styles over the years. Usually in plain silver, they also come with enameled handles, and, in the case of 36-4, with a semi-precious stone set in the handle. Tea strainers also come in a variety of forms. Some with two handles can be placed directly on the cup (36-5, right); the single-handled strainers can be held with one hand while the tea is poured with the other (36-5, left). Handles are of wood (36-6), ivory, and silver.

The silver tea ball is a 20th-century novelty which enables the server to steep the tea to the desired strength and then eaily remove the leaves. Not illustrated is the silver-plated spoon with a pierced bowl and cover that is used to make a single cup of tea.

36-0 Tea Caddy (color plate)
Tiffany & Co., Inc.
New York, New York, c. 1878
H. 4½"

Deep oblong box with a separate lid. A ball attached to the top by four curved rods forms the handle. The body decorated with a figure, bamboo, grasses, and other oriental motifs. Border of incised triangles at the top. At the bottom a stepped border with birds and leaves. **(A)**

The Burt Collection

36-1 Tea Caddy
Tiffany & Company
New York, New York, c. 1865
H. 6½"

Tea caddy with separate cast handles. Two hinged compartments with lids engraved with leaf patterns. Die-rolled borders. **(A)**

The Burt Collection

36-2 Tea Caddy (left)
Towle Silversmiths
Newburyport, Massachusetts, c. 1915
H. 5"

Circular ovoid-shaped body with a repoussé design of swirled scrolls at the bottom. Bulbous cover. **(C)**

Tea Caddy (right)
Towle Silversmiths
Newburyport, Massachusetts, c. 1915
H. 4½"

Circular bulbous body with a beaded rim. The domed lid terminates in a hemispherical finial. **(C)**

Towle catalogue, c. 1915

36-3 Tea Caddy Spoon
Tiffany & Co., Inc.
New York, New York, c. 1900
L. 3¾"

Heart-shaped bowl, the handle chased in a design of holly leaves and berries. **(B)**

The Burt Collection

36-4 Tea Caddy Spoon
Greif
c. 1940
L. 2¾"

Hand-hammered design in the Danish tradition with a moonstone set into the handle. Marked "GREIF." **(C)**

Author's Collection

36-5 Tea Strainer (left)
Tiffany & Co., Inc.
New York, New York, c. 1895
L. 6¾"

Tea strainer with an ivory handle. The strainer with a broad rim embossed with a design of leaves and flowers. **(B)**

Tea Strainer (right)
Tiffany & Co., Inc.
New York, New York, c. 1920
L. 5¾"

Two-handled tea strainer, the handles with egg-and-dart borders, the strainer with egg-and-dart borders and a design of scrolls. **(C)**

The Burt Collection

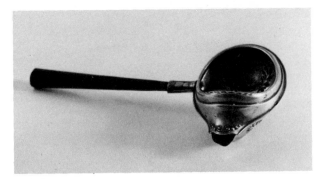

36-6 Tea Strainer
Paye & Baker Mfg. Co.
North Attleboro, Massachusetts, c. 1900
L. 6¾"

Oval strainer with the screened, scrolled spout at one side. Ebony handle. **(B)**

Private Collection

36-7 Tea Ball
Maker unknown
c. 1920
H. 2"

Tea ball in the shape of a teapot with a chain and ring handle. **(D)**

36-8 Tea Ball
Amcraft
Attleboro, Massachusetts, c. 1920
H. ⅞" (ball); D. 2" (drainer)

Tea ball in the shape of a teapot with chain and ring holder and a separate drainer. **(D)**

Private Collection

36-9 Tea Ball
Webster Company
North Attleboro, Massachusetts, c. 1920
D. 1¾"

Spherical tea ball with chain and ring holder. **(D)**

37 | Sugar Tongs

The first sugar tongs were made in the early 18th century. These early tongs, called nippers, are shaped like a pair of scissors and are used to pinch off a piece of sugar from a larger lump. Nineteenth-century American sugar tongs bear a close relation to the spoon, for they consist of two small bowls on long stems joined by an arch, which is tempered for spring and flexibility. This tension is required for the picking up of small lumps of sugar. Tongs are decorated simply with pierced, chased, and bright-cut embellishment. A typical fancy of the Victorian period, however, was to make the holders take the form of the claws of a bird (37-4, 37-5). The scallop-shell spoon bowl, a favorite motif of silversmiths (37-6), was popular during the first half of the 19th century and again during the Colonial Revival later in the century.

37-O Sugar Tongs (color plate)
Gorham & Company
Providence, Rhode Island, c. 1860
L. 6″

Two pairs of tongs in the Gorham "Medallion" pattern. The claw grips are identical, but one pair has the medallions on the sides of the handles, while on the other the medallions are located at the juncture of the handles. **(B)**

The Burt Collection

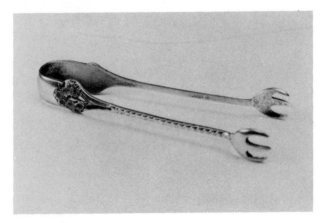

37-1 Sugar Tongs
Gorham Mfg. Company
Providence, Rhode Island, 1902
L. 3½″

Three-clawed tongs with the sides decorated with blue enameled flowers on green stems. **(B)**

The Burt Collection

37-2 Sugar Tongs
R. Wallace & Sons Mfg. Co.
Wallingford, Connecticut, c. 1920
L. 4¾″

Five-clawed tongs in hotel silver with "BPOE" on the sides. Silver-plated. **(D)**

37-3 Sugar Tongs
Gorham Mfg. Company
Providence, Rhode Island, c. 1920
L. 4¼″

Five-clawed tongs in Gorham's "Etruscan" pattern (see 12-2). **(D)**

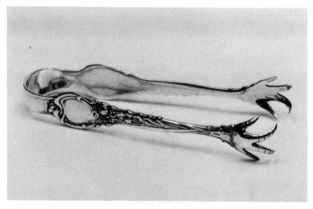

37-4 Sugar Tongs
Whiting Mfg. Co.
Providence, Rhode Island, c. 1910
L. 6½"

Four-clawed tongs, the shaped handles with a design of flowers and
ribbons in relief. **(C)**

Private Collection

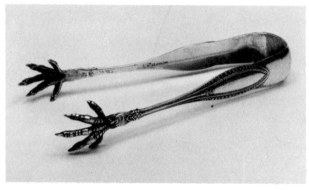

37-5 Sugar Tongs
Reed & Barton
Taunton, Massachusetts, c. 1890
L. 4¾"

Naturalistic five-toed bird's foot tongs. The sides of the handles
decorated with an oval beaded design. **(C)**

Private Collection

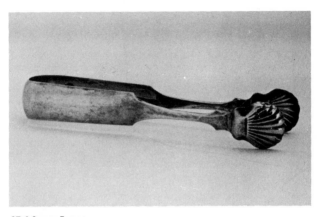

37-6 Sugar Tongs
S. Hildeburn
Philadelphia, Pennsylvania, c. 1835
L. 6"

Typical early-19th-century American tongs with scallop-shell bowls and straight, slightly convex handles. **(C)**

Author's Collection

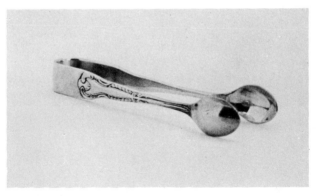

37-7 Sugar Tongs
Maker unknown, c. 1910
L. 4"

Tongs consisting of miniature spoons connected by a plain hoop, with the pattern that is usually on the top of the spoon on the reverse side. Silver-plated. **(D)**

Author's Collection

III AROUND THE HOUSE

38 | Candlesticks and Candelabra

The candlestick and the candelabrum have been in use since the Middle Ages, and continue in use today. Candlelight is romantic, the candle is relatively inexpensive, and the holder is a thing of beauty and grace. An ordinary candlestick consists of three parts: the base, the shaft, and the socket, which is often furnished with a saucer or bowl to catch the drippings (38-1). These are sometimes called nozzles or, if not part of the original, bobeches. The candelabrum is simply a candlestick furnished with a number of arms to accommodate several candles (38-5). These are removable so that the candles can be used elsewhere.

Early candlesticks consists of a flat pan and a conical stick on which the candle is impaled. By the 18th century the cylindrical socket was used for all but ecclesiastical purposes. Traditionally, the candlestick or candelabrum stands on a square, round, or oval base or plinth, depending on the period. The Victorians, for example, were highly imaginative in their design of candlesticks, sculpting figures of animals, cupids, and goddesses to hold the lamp aloft or merely to decorate the base. Plates 38-2 and 38-6 illustrate departures from the traditional form.

38-O Candlesticks (color plate)
Gorham Mfg. Company
Providence, Rhode Island, 1908
H. 8¾"

Typical "Martelé" Art Nouveau form (see 2-6), with undulating chased and engraved design of violets, the stems of which begin at the base and terminate just below the shaped socket. **(A)**

Private Collection

38-1 Candlesticks

Tiffany & Co., Inc.
New York, New York, c. 1900
H. 8¼"

Four candlesticks with removable nozzles. Each with four applied, die-rolled bands decorated with stylized cornucopia and scrolls. **(B)**

The Burt Collection

38-2 Candlesticks
Gorham Mfg. Company
Providence, Rhode Island, 1869
H. 7¼"

Pair of candlesticks with seated putti on a footed base holding rod stems which support urn-shaped holders with bird's head handles. **(B)**

The Burt Collection

38-3 Candlesticks
Gorham Mfg. Company
Providence, Rhode Island, 1914
H. 10¾"

Baluster-shaped candlesticks tapering to a stepped octagonal base. Rococo scrolled design. **(C)**

I. Freeman & Son
New York, NY

38-4 Candlesticks
Graff, Washbourne & Dunn
New York, New York, c. 1930
H. 13″

Baluster-shaped candlesticks flaring at the bottom to broad scroll bases. Nozzles with broad drip pans. Engraved scroll and bellflower designs on the shoulders and bases. **(C)**

I. Freeman & Son
New York, NY

38-5 Candelabrum
Meriden Britannia Company
Meriden, Connecticut, c. 1886
H. 13" approx.

Baluster-shaped candelabrum with fluted decoration on the base, nozzles, and joints. Available in three- and five-light forms. Silver-plated. **(C)**

Meriden B. catalogue, 1886
The International Silver Company Historical Library

38-6 Chamberstick
Gorham Mfg. Company
Providence, Rhode Island
c. 1888
H. 6" approx.

Chamberstick with the socket terminating in a cornucopia flanked by a bulldog. The whole on a chased rectangular base. Fingerhold on the side. **(B)**

Gorham catalogue, 1888

38-7 Candelabrum
Meriden Britannia Company
Meriden, Connecticut, 1886
H. 8" approx.

Two-light candelabrum with two bulbous sockets on thin stems flanking a standing figure on a base. The whole on scroll feet. Silver-plated. **(C)**

No. 115.

38-8 Candelabrum
Meriden Britannia Company
Meriden, Connecticut, c. 1886
H. 12"

Three-light candelabrum with a circular base on splayed feet. The tall center socket supported by two scrolls. The lower two lights at the base level. Silver-plated. **(C)**

Meriden B. catalogue, 1886. The International Silver Company Historical Library.

39 | Flower Vases and Bowls

Classic vases are composed of three simple forms or parts: the foot, the body, and the neck. Numerous variations are possible with the addition of a handle or handles, a lid, or a spout. The most important part, the body, is composed of basic shapes which find their prototypes in natural forms, such as eggs, fruit, or nut shapes, animal horns, and similar objects. Bases vary, but often consist of rim-foot pedestals. An unusual variation shows a squirrel seated on a sculpted base (39-9).

Flower bowls with pierced metal inserts for securing stems were popular in the 1920s and '30s (39-7). Low bowls of massed flowers took the place of the elaborate centerpieces and épergnes of the 19th century.

39-0 Vase (color plate)
Wood & Hughes
New York, New York, c. 1865
H. 9½"

Two-handled cylindrical vase-form body, the lobed base tapered on a stepped spreading rim pedestal. The body with cartouches in repoussé and chased on each side with roses at the top and anthemia at the sides and bottom. Cast handles in the form of phoenixes. **(B)**

Private Collection

39-1 Vase
Tiffany & Co., Inc.
New York, New York, 1892
H. 9"

Three-handled, urn-shaped body
—the scroll handles terminating in
square feet. The lower portion
lobed and the upper portion
decorated with chased and repoussé putti, flowers, and foliage.
(B)

The Burt Collection

39-2 Vase
Tiffany & Co., Inc.
New York, New York, 1903
H. 22"

Amphora-shaped, two-handled
vase. The neck and vase decorated with acanthus leaves; the circular foot with a border of palmettes. **(B)**

Collection of The Newark Museum
Newark, NJ

39-3 Vase (left)
Wood & Hughes
New York, New York, 1868
H. 8½"

Two-handled cylindrical vase-form body, the lobed base tapered on
a stepped spreading rim pedestal (see 36-1). The flaring strap handles
attached to the body with elaborate scrolls. **(B)**

Vase (right)
Gorham Mfg. Company
Providence, Rhode Island, 1865
H. 7"

Amphora-shaped, two-handled vase. The handles attached to the
body and below the rim with scrollwork. The whole on a tall slender
stem and a circular spreading foot. **(B)**

The Burt Collection

39-4 Vase
Tiffany & Co., Inc.
New York, New York, c. 1900
H. 17¾"

Vase-shaped cylindrical body with scroll handles on a stepped base. The body decorated with incised tendrils; the rim and the base gadrooned. Cast applied handles attached to the top with rosettes. **(A)**

Collection of The Newark Museum Newark, NJ

39-5 Vase
Tiffany & Co., Inc.
New York, New York, 1905
H. 3½"

Narrow-necked vase flaring sharply to a broad base with an overall incised design of violets. **(B)**

The Burt Collection

39-6 Flower Bowl
Tiffany & Co., Inc.
New York, New York, c. 1925
H. 3½"

Low, shallow flower bowl with a shaped, broad everted rim. Plate inset serves as a holder. **(B)**

39-7 Flower Bowl
Tiffany & Co., Inc.
New York, New York, c. 1930
H. 6"

Shallow circular bowl on a short pedestal with a spreading rim foot. The rim decorated with a floral border. Plate inset functions as a flower holder. **(C)**

The Burt Collection

39-8 Vase
Meriden Britannia Company
Meriden, Connecticut, c. 1886
H. 10" approx.

Ovoid vase chased with a pattern of flowers and birds on a matte background. Silver-plated. **(C)**

Meriden B. catalogue, 1886
The International Silver Company
Historical Library.

39-10 Vase
Reed & Barton
Taunton, Massachusetts, c. 1884
H. 9" approx.

Cylindrical vase on a spreading foot. The decorative handles formed of stag heads and buds. **(C)**

39-9 Vase
Simpson, Hall, Miller & Co.
Wallingford, Connecticut
c. 1890
H. 9¾"

Circular opaque glass insert in a base supported by vines and tendrils rising from a sculptured base with a seated squirrel. Silver-plated. **(B)**

Private Collection

39-11 Vase
Meriden Britannia Company
Meriden, Connecticut, c. 1910
H. 14⅞"

Trumpet-shaped vase on a domed foot. Everted, perforated rim. Silver-plated. **(C)**

Collection of Mr. & Mrs. Theodore Rockafellow
New Britain, PA

39-12 Vase
Meriden Britannia Company
Meriden, Connecticut, c. 1886
H. 8" approx.

Concave cylindrical vase held in a frame that forms a base. Open handles. Chased decoration. Silver-plated. **(C)**

No. 61.

39-13 Vase
Meriden Britannia Company
Meriden, Connecticut, c. 1886
H. 9" approx.

Square-shaped colored glass vase with a scalloped rim. Square base on four cast feet in the shape of turtles. Silver-plated. **(C)**

Meriden B. catalogue, 1886
The International Silver Company
Historical Library.

39-14 Vase
Maker unknown
c. 1920
H. 8"

Three-footed scroll base holding a tall shaped vase in the center. Three similarly shaped smaller vases held diagonally in the base. **(C)**

40 | Trophies

A silver trophy has long been a desirable prize for all kinds of competitions and achievements. Many of the major sports competitions today take their name from the trophy presented to the winner: the Walker Cup in golf, the Davis Cup in tennis, the Stanley Cup in hockey, and the America's Cup in yachting. The word "trophy" comes from the Greek for a memorial of victory set up on the field of battle at the spot where the enemy had been routed.

If the trophy is a loving cup, or two-handled vase form, champagne is traditionally drunk from it; if it is an imposing edifice of some sort, it is usually hoisted aloft and paraded around the arena by the winning team. In addition to the special order trophies to which engraved names of winners are added over the years, the 19th-century silver companies offered standard trophies for winners and competitors in many sports. Often a basic or standard shape is simply surmounted by a figure engaged in whatever sport is being honored (40-3). An even more common stock item was available with a draped figure offering a laurel wreath. The competition honored was then engraved to order on the side.

Silver trophies are most valuable for their intrinsic metallic worth. Silver-plated trophies are curiosities, for the most part, and have little other than a sentimental value to the presentee or his family.

40-0 Trophy (color plate)
Reed & Barton
Taunton, Massachusetts, c. 1890
H. 9¾"

Circular concave cup with scroll handles on a baluster stem and a domed foot. The stem decorated with crossed rackets. Silver-plated. **(C)**

Reed & Barton Collection

40-1 Trophy
R. Wallace & Sons Mfg. Co.
Wallingford, Connecticut, 1931
H. 16½"

Cylindrical vase form with scroll handles. The shoulder and the spreading rim foot decorated with a border of leaves and flowers. **(C)**

Private Collection

40-2 Trophy
Towle Silversmiths
Newburyport, Massachusetts,
c. 1915
H. 10" approx.

Three-handled trophy or loving cup. The ovoid body with a shaped rim. The handles swirl from top to bottom. The base decorated with flowers and foliage. **(C)**

Towle catalogue, c. 1915.

40-3 Bicycling Trophy
Meriden Britannia Company
Meriden, Connecticut, c. 1886
H. 14" approx.

Ovoid body on a baluster stem and spreading rim foot. Scroll handles with decorative loops extending to the base. Engraved figure of a cyclist in a circular cartouche. The whole surmounted with a sculptured figure of a cyclist and his bicycle. Silver-plated. **(C)**

Meriden B. catalogue, 1886
The International Silver Company Historical Library.

40-4 Skating Trophy
Meriden Britannia Company
Meriden, Connecticut, c. 1886
H. 12" approx.

Cylindrical, flaring vase-shaped body with a rounded bottom on a spreading rim foot. Handles of buds and stems with rosettes. Cartouche with engraved figure of a skater on a stippled background. Silver-plated. **(C)**

Meriden B. catalogue, 1886
The International Silver Company Historical Library.

40-5 Horse Racing Trophy
Meriden Britannia Company
Meriden, Connecticut, c. 1886
H. 14" approx.

Cylindrical, tapering covered cup on a baluster stem with a spreading rim foot; cast, applied scrollwork on the stem. The whole surmounted by the figure of a jockey. Silver-plated. **(C)**

Meriden B. catalogue, 1886
The International Silver Company
Historical Library

41 | Card Receivers

Life in the 19th century was considerably more formal than today. Women of the middle and upper classes enjoyed the luxury of servants, who performed the housework and freed these women to make calls on friends. Women were also likely to have a morning or afternoon "at home" each week and were required to observe other complicated social rituals. All of these factors contributed to the popularity of the card receiver, a kind of plate for depositing these calling cards.

The use of the card and the formal call was not restricted to women either, since men also "left" cards. The card receiver was the one piece of silver seen by each caller and silver companies vied with each other to provide some extraordinary examples of the manufacturers' art. These receivers were meant to be seen and commented upon. They range from the simple salver (41-1) to elaborate pieces which tell a story (41-4), like the plaster Rogers groups of the period. Additionally, the receiver might incorporate a piece of ornamental sculpture or a simple vase for flowers (41-5).

The relaxed atmosphere of society following World War I resulted in the abandonment of the card receiver in all but the most traditional of homes. Today these objects are highly valued as collectibles and almost any one of them in good condition can find an honored place on a side table or on the dining table as a centerpiece.

41-O Card Receiver (color plate)
Maker unknown
c. 1885
H. 12"

Flat hexagonal tray with rustic handles on a tall stem decorated with cattails and leaves. Cast base with four cutouts. Silver-plated. **(C)**

Private Collection

41-1 Card Receiver
Tiffany & Co., Inc.
New York, New York, c. 1932
5⅛" square

Square tray divided into quadrants by crossed diagonal pattern of incised broken lines and scrolls. **(C)**

The Burt Collection

41-2 Card Receiver
W. & S. Blackinton Co.
Meriden, Connecticut, c. 1925
D. 7¼"

Circular plate on four scroll feet. Gadrooned border and engraved

decoration of scrolls and foliage surrounding a monogram. **(C)**

Private Collection

41-3 Card Receiver
Meriden Britannia Company
Meriden, Connecticut, c. 1886
L. 5" approx.

Shaped dish on four splayed feet, the handle forms a morning-glory blossom and stem. Silver-plated. **(C)**

Meriden B. catalogue, 1886
The International Silver Company
Historical Library

41-4 Card Receiver

Middletown Plate Co.
Middletown, Connecticut, c. 1885
H. 6"

Shallow circular dish which simulates wooden planks. The tollkeeper at one end tries to exact a kiss as toll for his bridge. Silver-plated. **(B)**

Private Collection

41-5 Card Receiver
Reed & Barton
Taunton, Massachusetts, c. 1884
H. 10" approx.

Combination card receiver and vase. The stationary open bail handles with cherubs at either side terminate with a trumpet-shaped vase on a pedestal; set on an octagonal base. Silver-plated. **(C)**

Reed & Barton catalogue, 1884

41-6 Card Receiver
Rogers & Bro.
Waterbury, Connecticut, c. 1890
H. 6¾"

A cherub astride the stem of a lily pad, guiding it with reins. The pad on a scroll-and-flower base. Silver-plated. **(B)**

Private Collection

41-7 Card Receiver
Meriden Britannia Company
Meriden, Connecticut, c. 1886
H. 3" approx.

Diamond-shaped hammered dish on a circular base. The edge decorated with flowers and leaves. The handle composed of bound stems. Silver-plated. **(C)**

Meriden B. catalogue, 1886
The International Silver Company Historical Library

41-8 Card Receiver
Derby Silver Co.
Derby, Connecticut, c. 1895
L. 12" approx.

Card receiver in the shape of a fan with an elaborate engraved design in the Japanese style. Receiver stands on turtle feet. Silver-plated. **(C)**

Derby catalogue, c. 1895
The International Silver Company Historical Library

42 | Desk Accessories

Matching desk sets consisting of blotter corners, a paper knife, letter opener, stamp box, calendar, etc., were made for both men and women in silver. The desk, however, was primarily the man's province and most of the sets made from the 1890s to the 1920s have a decidedly masculine flavor. A 1904 catalogue lists the following pieces as being available in sterling silver: stationery rack, pen tray, letter clip, paper knife (42-7), pen wiper, pen stand (42-3), mucilage bottle, bill file, blotter, stamp box (42-8), tape measure, letter opener (42-4), ink eraser, sealing wax set, sealing wax ladle, seal (42-6), candlestick, moistener, shears, inkstand, twine holder (42-9), check cutter, match vase, calendar and picture frames (42-10), and blotter corners. The most common 19th-century desk accessory was a holder for ink (42-2), although the fountain pen usurped its place in the early years of this century. A full complement of these objects would leave little room for working space, but a few of these items were sufficient to give a rich look to the library desk.

42-0 Inkstand (color plate)
Meriden Britannia Company
Meriden, Connecticut, c. 1876
L. 7¾"

Rectangular tray with gently curving sides decorated with beading and shells, four ball feet. Pressed glass inkwells on round stems fit into stationary holders. The rims of the covers are beaded and centered with a red, white, and blue inset, possibly as a tribute to our nation's centenary in 1876. Silver-plated. **(B)**

Author's Collection

42-1 Inkwell
Gorham Mfg. Company
Providence, Rhode Island, 1895
H. 2"

Square crystal inkwell with hinged silver top. Monogrammed in a circular beaded cartouche surrounded by swags. **(C)**

No. 36.

42-2 Inkwell
Meriden Britannia Company
Meriden, Connecticut, c. 1886
H. 4½" approx.

Owl on perch mounted on an engraved pedestal with splayed feet. Pen rest on the base. Silver-plated. **(B)**

Meriden B. catalogue, 1886
The International Silver Company
Historical Library

42-3 Pen Rack
Maker unknown
c. 1890
L. 5"

Long oval base decorated with flowers, foliage, and scrolls. **(C)**

Author's Collection

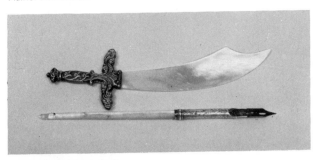

42-4 Letter Opener (top)
Codding Bros. & Heilborn
North Attleboro, Massachusetts, c. 1900
L. 6"

Mother-of-pearl scimitar letter opener with a silver handle. Repoussé foliage and vines decorate the handle. **(C)**

Pen (bottom)
Maker unknown
c. 1890
L. 6"

Dip pen with a mother-of-pearl shaft and silver mountings elaborately etched. **(C)**

Private Collection

42-5 Letter Opener
Gorham Mfg. Company
Providence, Rhode Island, 1900
L. 6½"

Steel letter opener with a repoussé handle in a lily design. **(C)**

Private Collection

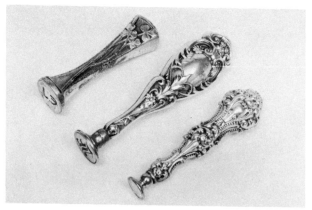

42-6 Seal (left)
Maker unknown
c. 1900
L. 2⅝"

Art Nouveau decorations of shamrocks and stems adorn handle. Silver-plated. **(C)**

Seal (center)
Maker unknown
c. 1890
L. 3⅞"

Scroll, leaf, and flower decoration adorns handle. **(C)**

Seal (right)
Maker unknown

c. 1895
L. 3⅝"

Floral and foliage decoration with beaded outlines adorns shaft. **(C)**

Private Collection

42-7 Paper Cutter
Tiffany & Co., Inc.
New York, New York, c. 1893
L. 11½"

Rectangular form chased with a view of the Mines and Mining Pavilion at the Columbian Exposition, 1893. Heart-shaped handle decorated with an Art Nouveau design of scrolls and leaves. Tiffany's mark includes a globe indicating that the piece was made for the exposition.
(A)

Lyndhurst Corporation
New York, NY

42-8 Stamp Box
Theodore B. Starr
New York, New York, c. 1905
L. 2"

Rectangular hinged box; the top with a design of shells, flowers, and foliage in repoussé. **(C)**

The Burt Collection

**42-9 Twine Holder
Gorham Mfg. Company
Providence, Rhode Island, 1895
H. 3¾"**

Bulbous form, the top perforated and decorated with acanthus leaves, the bottom fluted on a straight foot. **(B)**

The Burt Collection

42-10 Calendar Frame (left)
**Tiffany & Co., Inc.
New York, New York, c. 1920
L. 3¾"**

Rectangular calendar frame with the monogram "VMB" at top center. **(C)**

Picture frame (right)
**Tiffany & Co., Inc.
New York, New York c. 1920
L. 3¾"**

Plain square frame with a ring at the top. The picture opening forms an oval. Initials "MEB" at the bottom right corner. **(C)**

The Burt Collection

43 | Smoking Accessories

The smoking accessories of the 19th century were designed largely for use by men. Those avant-garde women who smoked did so in the privacy of their boudoirs. The Gorham catalogue for 1898 pictures cigar cases, cigarette cases (43-2), cigar cutters, cigar lighters, snuff boxes, pipe cleaners, and tobacco boxes. Although table lighters and hammered copper ashtrays existed in the 19th century, it was not until the 20th century that these accessories became popular in silver. Humidors—containers designed to keep tobacco products moist—were often made of cut or pressed glass with silver tops (43-5).

43-O Table Lighter (color plate, left)
Tiffany & Co., Inc.
New York, New York, c. 1935
H. 3¾"

Octagonal, tapered table lighter on an octagonal base. **(C)**

Cigar Box (color plate, right)
Tiffany & Co., Inc.
New York, New York, c. 1935
H. 3½"

Oblong cigar box. The only decoration is a cast, applied floral motif in the upper left corner. **(C)**

I. Freeman & Son
New York, NY

43-1 Ashtray
Tiffany & Co., Inc.
New York, New York, c. 1930
D. 3½"

Circular, shallow ashtray with twelve tapered panels. **(C)**

The Burt Collection

43-2 Cigarette Case
Bennet-Merwin Silver Co.
New Milford, Connecticut,
    c. 1915
L. 3⅜"

Rectangular cigarette case with rounded corners. Overall decoration of flowers and foliage. Diamond-shaped cartouche for intials. Gilt interior with spring retainers on both sides to hold cigarettes. **(C)**

Author's Collection

43-3 Cigarette Urn
Maker unknown
c. 1940
H. 3¼"

Classic urn-shaped cigarette holder with double handles. Gadrooned rim and spreading foot. **(D)**

Private Collection

43-4 Smoking Set
Wm. B. Kerr & Co.
Newark, New Jersey, c. 1900
D. 8" (tray); H. 2¾", 2⅝", 1¾" (urns); H. ⅝" (ashtray)

Five-piece smoking set. Shaped tray with a crocus and stem border. Each of the other pieces with repoussé crocuses and stems. **(B)**

Collection of The Newark Museum
Newark, NJ

43-5 Humidor
Maker unknown
c. 1900
H. 7"

Octagonal glass humidor with a silver top decorated with morning-glories. **(C)**

Private Collection

43-6 Cigar Clipper/Match
  Holder/Ashtray
Derby Silver Co.
Derby, Connecticut, c. 1885

No. 23. For 50 Cigars.

H. 4½"

Combined match holder, cigar cutter, and ashtray. A combination of useful items such as this is characteristic of the late-Victorian period. A naturalistic bird stands beside the ashtray, giving it more weight. Silver-plated. **(B)**

Collection of Mr. & Mrs. Theodore Rockafellow
New Britain, PA

43-7 Cigar Box
Meriden Britannia Company
Meriden, Connecticut, 1886.
H. 9" approx.

Heavily chased rectangular cigar box for 50 cigars. The cyclist on the top was probably also used on trophies. Silver-plated. **(B)**

Meriden B. catalogue, 1886
The International Silver Company
Historical Library

IV PERSONAL ACCESSORIES

44 | Toilet and Boudoir Accessories

Elaborate matching toilet sets in silver date back to the early 17th century in England, but in the United States they did not appear on the scene until well into the 19th century. Not until the emergence of a well-to-do middle class was there the time or the money for any but the wealthiest women to spend on their toilets. Then the floodgates opened. Each new catalogue offered more tools, bottles, and jars. An 1886 catalogue, for instance, featured cream boxes, scissors, a nail file, buffer, cuticle knife, corn knife, glove button hook, and shoe button hook for milady. A 1910 catalogue included all of the above, as well as vinaigrettes for smelling salts, a comb, toothbrush, toothbrush tube, talcum powder bottle, shoehorn, hairpin box, tweezers, nail clippers, glove stretchers, puff knob with puff, hat pin vase, and pin cushion. All of these are in sterling.

The most interesting decorative motifs developed over the years for tiolet and boudoir accessories are the repoussé versions of flowers and naiads especially favored in the Art Nouveau period. They are back in favor today and highly collectible. The Unger Brothers catalogue for 1900 shows toilet sets in the following Art Nouveau patterns: "Le Secretes des Fleurs," "He loves Me," "Reine des Fleurs," "Dawn," "Love's Dream," "Evangeline," "Art Nouveau," "Cupid," "Tulip," and "Water Lily." Seventy-seven items were available in the "Cupid" pattern alone.

The advent of beauty parlors during the 1920s saw the flood of toilet articles reduced to a trickle as those women who could afford all the tools and bottles could also pay the cost of visiting the beauty parlor regularly. It was back to the essentials again for the manufacturers, and a typical set from the '20s consists of only a comb and brush, a hand mirror, a powder box, and a few manicure implements.

44-O Boudoir Set (color plate)
Tiffany & Co., Inc.
New York, New York, c. 1920
L. (clockwise from lower left): button hook 6"; nail file 6¾"; pin tray 6"; mirror 8"; clothes brush 5⅞"; hairbrush 5"; and scissors 3¼"

A simple, unadorned boudoir set, the only decorations are incised line borders on all pieces. **(C)**

I. Freeman & Son
New York, NY

44-2 Chatelaine Clip
Wm. B. Kerr
Newark, New Jersey, c. 1890
L. 1⅞"

Chatelaine clip with a design of shells and scrolls and cupid's head in the center. **(C)**

Collection of The Newark Museum Newark, NJ

44-1 Soap Dish
Unger Bros.
Newark, New Jersey, c. 1900
L. 3½"

Soap dish in Unger's "Love's Dream" pattern. In 1904 Unger listed seventy-one other toilet items in the same pattern. **(C)**

Collection of The Newark Museum Newark, NJ

44-3 Powder Jar
Maker unknown
c. 1900
H. 3½"

Pressed glass bulbous jar with a silver lid in a typical Art Nouveau design. **(C)**

Private Collection

44-4 Nail File/Cuticle Knife
Maker unknown
c. 1897
L. 5½"

Steel nail file and cuticle knife with swirling, fluted hollow handle of silver. **(C)**

Author's Collection

44-5 Nail Buffer (top)
Maker unknown
c. 1905
L. 4"

Nail buffer with grip handle. Scroll and leaf decoration. **(C)**

Manicure Scissors (below)
Maker unknown
c. 1900
L. 4½"

Manicure scissors with rococo silver handles. **(C)**

Cuticle Tool (below)
Maker unknown
c. 1900
L. 4¾"

Cuticle tool with an ebony handle and silver mountings. **(C)**

Cuticle Tool and Nail File (bottom)
Maker unknown
c. 1900
L. 5½" (tool); L. 6¾" (file)

Matching cuticle tool and nail file with scroll and flower decorations. Both pieces with the monogram "CEH." **(C)**

Private Collection

44-6 Nail Buffer (top)
The McChesney Co.
Newark, New Jersey, c. 1925
L. 6¼"

Long oval nail buffer, the handle initialed and the body decorated with an egg-and-dart border. **(C)**

Nail Buffer (bottom)
R. Wallace & Sons Mfg. Co.
Wallingford, Connecticut, c. 1920
L. 5½"

Long oval nail buffer with an oblong handle. Hand-hammered overall. **(C)**

Private Collection

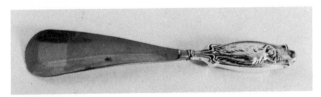

44-7 Shoehorn
Maker unknown
c. 1900
L. 7"

Shoehorn, the silver handle decorated with a transparently draped female figure. **(D)**

Author's Collection

44-8 Vinaigrette (standing)
Whiting Mfg. Co.
Providence, Rhode Island,
  c. 1900
H. 3"

Pressed glass cylindrical bottle with a hinged silver top; the top repoussé with flowers. **(C)**

Vinaigrette (left)
Maker unknown
c. 1900
H. 3¾"

Circular, tapered pressed glass bottle with a hinged silver top. A wreath of flowers surrounds a monogram on top. Silver-plated. **(C)**

Vinaigrette (right)
Maker unknown
c. 1900
H. 3¾"

Circular, tapered pressed glass bottle with a hexagonal bottom. Hinged silver top with scrolled and beaded border enclosing a monogram. **(C)**

Private Collection

44-9 Toothbrush Holder (left)
Maker unknown
c. 1905
H. 7"

Toothbrush holder with a fluted and ridged glass body and a silver screw top decorated with a wreath of flowers. **(C)**

Toothbrush Holder (right)
Maker unknown
c. 1905
H. 7⅛"

Toothbrush holder with an octagonal glass body and a silver screw top. The top and the matching toothbrush decorated with lilies of the valley. **(C)**

Private Collection

44-10 Pin Tray
Whiting Mfg. Co.
Newark, New Jersey, c. 1900
L. 4⅜"

Oval tray, the flaring sides formed by naturalistic repoussé fiddle ferns. **(C)**

Private Collection

45 | Hand Mirrors

First place in the pantheon of ladies' toilet articles belongs to the hand mirror. In 1835 the process of "silvering" glass to give it the properties of a mirror was perfected, and five years later the manufacture of the mirror as we know it today was begun. The hand mirror was an integral part of the toilet set and enjoyed a popularity of its own during the period of elaborate hair styles. These styles could only be perfected with the use of a mirror that reflected the back of the head in a dressing table mirror. During the early part of the 20th century, Art Nouveau designs for mirrors were the most popular. In the 1920s and '30s, however, the mirrors had longer handles and the decoration was far more discreet, often with a simple engraved border or neoclassical styling.

45-0 Hand Mirror (color plate)
Maker unknown
c. 1905
L. 9"

Mirror surmounted by a profile of a woman whose strands of hair trail down on both sides, creating a border. **(C)**

Private Collection

45-1 Hand Mirror
Unger Bros.
Newark, New Jersey, c. 1905
L. 10"

Hand mirror outlined with scroll-work which frames a woman's profile and daisies in the "He Loves Me" pattern. **(C)**

Collection of The Newark Museum Newark, NJ

45-2 Hand Mirror
Gorham Mfg. Company
Providence, Rhode Island, 1898
L. 10"

Hand mirror with naturalistic lilies forming a border around a mono-gram. **(C)**

Private Collection

45-3 Hand Mirror
Maker unknown
c. 1910
L. 9½"

Overall design of flowers and foliage surrounding a scroll-framed cartouche in the center. **(C)**

45-4 Hand Mirror
Maker unknown
c. 1905
L. 10"

Hand mirror with a shaped outline decorated with wild roses and foliage surrounding a monogram. **(C)**

Private Collection

45-5 Hand Mirror
Wm. Bens Co., Inc.
Providence, Rhode Island, c. 1918
L. 11"

Shield-shaped hand mirror with a shaped handle. A border of flowers and foliage centered with a palmette. **(C)**

Private Collection

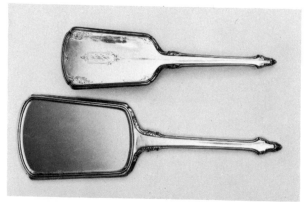

45-6 Hand Mirror and Brush
Wiley-Crawford Co., Inc.
Newark, New Jersey, c. 1920
L. 13⅛" (mirror); L. 10¼" (brush)

Oblong mirror and brush set with long handles terminating in trefoils.
Narrow reeded borders with scrolls and foliage. **(C)**

Private Collection

45-7 Hand Mirror and Brush
R. Wallace & Sons Mfg. Co.
Wallingford, Connecticut, c. 1930
L. 13¼" (mirror); L. 9¼" (brush)

Long oval mirror and brush set with tapered handles. Danish motif of
stylized scrolls. **(C)**

46 | Perfume Bottles and Containers

Perfume bottles are usually of glass, either pressed in elaborate patterns or cut in an equally opulent manner. Since the tops of these bottles are relatively small, they are usually fashioned in sterling rather than silver plate, with repoussé floral designs predominating. In some cases, such as the bottle shown in 46-4, the entire glass container and stopper are covered with silver.

In addition to bottles made to hold perfume or cologne, the late-Victorian household could be supplied with an assortment of related items. Among these are cologne atomizers, cologne and toilet water flasks for traveling, bottle stands, lavender salts jars, and vinaigrettes. All of these were designed to be carried in the purse or placed on the dressing table.

46-O Perfume Bottle (color plate, left)
Gorham Mfg. Company
Providence, Rhode Island, c. 1902
H. 5"

Vase-shaped bottle with a domed lid, the body decorated with branches, leaves, and blossoms. The lid decorated similarly. **(C)**

Perfume Bottle (center)
Maker unknown
c. 1900
H. 1¾"

Rectangular plain flagon for the purse with screw top. **(C)**

Perfume Bottle (right)
Maker unknown
c. 1900
H. 3½"

Cylindrical bottle with incised borders at top and bottom. The lid hinged with a clasp. **(C)**

The Burt Collection

46-1 Perfume Bottle
Tiffany & Co., Inc.
New York, New York, c. 1900
L. 4½"

Amphora-shaped perfume bottle. The body and top covered with repoussé ferns and flowers. The top attached to the body with a chain. **(C)**

Collection of The Newark Museum
Newark, NJ

46-2 Perfume Bottle in Silver Case
Dominic & Haff, for Tiffany & Co., Inc.
New York, New York, c. 1900
L. 4¼"

Cylindrical case for glass perfume bottle. The bell-shaped screw top

and the body are decorated with repoussé flowers and foliage. **(B)**

Collection of The Newark Museum
Newark, NJ

46-3 Perfume Bottle
Unger Bros.
Newark, New Jersey, c. 1900
L. 4¾"

Tapered pressed glass bottle with a hinged silver top decorated with repoussé roses and leaves. Gilt lined. This form was also used for vinaigrettes (see 44-8). **(C)**

Author's Collection

46-4 Pair of Perfume Bottles
George W. Shiebler & Co.
New York, New York, c. 1898
H. 5¼"

Tall bottles with long, narrow necks, domed tops, and circular bulbous bodies. Leaves and scrolls outline a cartouche with "Odette" engraved within. Made for Shreve, Crump, & Low Company, Boston, by Shiebler. **(B)**

Ren's Antiques
Newtown, PA

46-5 Perfume Bottle
Maker unknown
c. 1910
H. 3"

Bulbous glass bottle with stopper and a silver overlay in a scroll design. **(D)**

Author's Collection

46-6 Perfume Bottle
Maker unknown
c. 1915
H. 5½"

Tall, pear-shaped green glass bottle with a silver overlay in a scroll design. **(C)**

Ren's Antiques
Newtown, PA

47 | **Brushes and Combs**

The silver comb-and-brush set was an extremely popular gift item in the early 20th century. A woman's crowning glory was her hair, and at a time before bobbing came into vogue, it required extensive brushing and combing. As mentioned previously in the section on boudoir accessories (see chapter 44), many of these brush sets were embellished with elaborate decorations of repoussé flowers and naiads (47-1). Combs were made of a combination of tortoise shell with silver mountings to match those of the brushes.

In addition to the hair brush, the silver manufacturer created brushes for every imaginable use. An early 20th-century catalogue lists eyebrow brushes, hat brushes, hat band brushes, hat rim brushes, mustache brushes, nail brushes, shaving brushes, tooth brushes, velvet brushes, and whisk brooms.

47-O Clothes Brush (color plate, top)
R. Blackinton & Co.
North Attleboro, Massachusetts, c. 1925
L. 6⅛"

Long, oval, silver-backed clothes brush with artificial bristles in a wooden base. Reeded border with clusters of flowers. **(C)**

Clothes Brush (bottom)
Gorham Mfg. Company
Providence, Rhode Island, c. 1910
L. 6¾"

Oblong, silver-backed clothes brush with an engraved border of scrolls and flowers. Natural bristles in a plastic base. **(C)**

Author's Collection

47-1 Clothes Brush (top)
Maker unknown
c. 1900
L. 6¼"

Oblong, silver-backed clothes brush with woman's head with flowing hair in tendrils and a floral pattern at the other end (see 45-0). **(C)**

Hair Brush (bottom)
Maker unknown
c. 1900
L. 8⅜"

Woman's silver-backed hair brush with handle. Same pattern as the clothes brush. **(C)**

Private Collection

47-2 Pair of Clothes Brushes
Maker unknown
c. 1900
L. 6¾"

Long, oblong, silver-backed clothes brushes with gently curving sides
and ends. A pattern of day lilies and foliage borders the cartouches.
(C)

47-3 Clothes Brush
Maker unknown
c. 1905
L. 7"

Oblong, silver-backed clothes brush with a pattern of morning-glories
and vines. Natural bristles in a plastic base. **(C)**

47-4 Clothes Brush
Maker unknown
c. 1905
L. 6"

Narrow, oblong, silver-backed clothes brush in the same pattern as
47-3.

47-5 Hair Brush
Unger Bros.
Newark, New Jersey, c. 1905
L. 8½"

Long-handled woman's hair brush
with an oval silver backing in
Unger's "He Loves Me" pattern of
a woman's head in profile with a
daisy design. (See also 45-1.) **(C)**

Collection of The Newark Museum
Newark, NJ

47-6 Hat Brush (left)
Maker unknown
c. 1900
L. 5¾"

Wide, silver-handled hat brush with a flower and foliage design. **(C)**

Hat Brush (right)
Maker unknown
c. 1900
L. 6¾"

Hat brush with a design of morning-glories and vines. **(C)**

Private Collection

47-7 Clothes Brush
Unger Bros.
Newark, New Jersey, c. 1900
L. 4⅜"

Oval, silver-backed clothes brush with a floral design. **(C)**

Collection of The Newark Museum
Newark, NJ

47-8 Comb and Brush Set
Gorham Mfg. Company
Providence, Rhode Island, c. 1925
L. 6¼" (brush); L. 6¾" (comb)

Man's silver-backed brush and comb set. The brush with a short handle. The tortoise shell comb with a silver mounting. Pigskin case (not shown). **(C)**

Author's Collection

47-9 Comb
R. Wallace & Sons Mfg. Co.
Wallingford, Connecticut, c. 1930
L. 7⅛"

Silver-mounted tortoise shell comb with scroll designs at both ends. **(D)**

Private Collection

47-10 Comb
Wiley-Crawford Co., Inc.
Newark, New Jersey, c. 1920
L. 7½"

Silver-mounted tortoise shell comb with stepped ends and a floral design in the center. **(D)**

47-11 Comb
R. Wallace & Sons Mfg. Co.
Wallingford, Connecticut, c. 1925
L. 7¼"

Silver-mounted tortoise shell comb with scroll and foliage decorations in the center and at the ends. **(D)**

48 | Shaving Accessories

Shaving accessories were the most common manly articles fashioned in silver and silver plate. Razors are sometimes mounted in silver, with the most elaborate of these containing seven razors, one for each day of the week. A similar unique device designed for traveling consists of a shaving brush that telescopes into a tube with a convenient cover. Razor strops are also silver-mounted, often designed for hanging, but also available with a shorter strop that fits into a silver case (48-5).

The shaving mugs featured in this section are embellished with simple decorations of reeding (48-1) and beading (48-2) along the borders. These mugs also feature a rest or lip to prevent the brush from slipping into the lather while shaving.

48-0 Shaving Mug (color plate)
Gorham Mfg. Company
Providence, Rhode Island, 1902
H. 2⁹/₁₆"

Cylindrical cup with engraved daffodils and leaves. Scroll strap handle gadrooned inside. Gilt-lined interior with brush holder. **(B)**

The Burt Collection

48-1 Shaving Mug
Derby Silver Co.
Derby, Connecticut, c. 1890
H. 2¼"

Concave cylindrical cup holder with a straight handle and brush holder. The openwork in a Gothic arch and scroll pattern. **(C)**

Private Collection

48-2 Shaving Mug
Gorham Mfg. Company
Providence, Rhode Island,
**   c. 1900**
H. 3"

Concave cylindrical cup with a
gadrooned harp handle. The rim
with three rows of stamped beading. Brush drainer insert. Silver-
plated. **(C)**

Private Collection

48-3 Shaving Mug
The Pairpoint Corporation
New Bedford, Massachusetts,
**   c. 1880**
H. 3¾"

Tapered cylindrical cup, broadly
lobed, flared at the rim. Cast, applied scroll handle. Insert for soap
and a brush holder. Silver-plated.
(C)

Collection of Mr. & Mrs. Theodore
Rockafellow
New Britain, PA

48-4 Shaving Mirror
Meriden Britannia Company
Meriden, Connecticut, c. 1886
H. 14" approx.

Tilting beveled mirror in a footed
silver frame decorated in the
"Eastlake Style." Silver-plated. **(C)**

Meriden B. catalogue, 1886
The International Silver Company
Historical Library

48-5 Razor Strop and Case
Tiffany & Co., Inc.
New York, New York, c. 1890
L. 12½"

Silver-handled razor strop, the leather portion fitting into a rectangular
silver case embossed with swirls and foliage. **(B)**

49 | Match Safes

Prior to the invention of book matches, the safety match was an essential item for the smoker, or even for a nonsmoker who occasionally required a light. Silver match safes provided a safe, almost waterproof, attractive carrier for these matches. The safes come in a variety of styles and were often made to look like miniatures of some common item. Illustration 49-0 shows a match safe made to look like a book, with the underside roughened to provide a scratcher for the match. From examples such as 49-1, which shows a patented match safe with a slide that opens and closes at the end, it is easy to see how these match safe forms became the precursor of the modern cigarette lighter. Larger match safes were also fashioned for home use to accommodate kitchen matches.

49-O Match Safe (color plate)
C. E. Barker Mfg. Co.
New York, New York, c. 1905
L. 1 ⅞"

Book-shaped match safe which opens like a book. Scratcher on the side and a ring at the top. **(C)**

Private Collection

49-1 Match Safe
Maker unknown
c. 1910
L. 2⅜"

Match safe with a sliding device on the top that opens one end. Scratcher on the opposite end. Silver-plated. **(C)**

Collection of Mr. & Mrs. Theodore Rockafellow
New Britain, PA

49-2 Match Safe
Unger Bros.
Newark, New Jersey, c. 1890
L. 2½"

Match safe with rococo design of scrolls and flowers. Hinged lid. **(C)**

Collection of The Newark Museum Newark, NJ

49-3 Match Safe
Stone Sterling Silver Co.
New York, New York, c. 1900
L. 2⅞"

Match safe with scrolled borders. Grotesque masks on hinged lid. Striker on the bottom. **(C)**

Ren's Antiques
Newtown, PA

49-4 Match Safe
Maker unknown
c. 1910
L. 2½"

Match safe with narrow leaf and scroll borders. Initialed. Hinged top. **(C)**

Ren's Antiques
Newtown, PA

49-5 Match Safe
Gorham Mfg. Company
Providence, Rhode Island,
   c. 1888
L. 2½"

Match safe with a design of U.S. coins in relief. Hinged lid. **(C)**

Gorham catalogue, 1888

50 | Boxes

Boxes in silver and silver plate come in a wide variety of shapes and sizes, ranging from the smallest hair pin boxes to the largest boxes made to contain jewelry. The standard boudoir set (50-5) consists of three pieces—a jewelry box, a glove box, and a handkerchief box. Jewelry boxes, or caskets, are the most common and are often elaborately decorated with repoussé or chased engraving. These boxes were popular from the 1890s until the 1930s. Since many are made of silver plate and have been subjected to constant handling, it is difficult to find them today in a condition suitable for everyday use.

50-O Pair of Boxes (color plate)
Maker unknown
c. 1900
D. 1⅝"

Circular silver boxes, the tops with borders of scrolls and flowers. **(C)**

Private Collection

50-1 Boudoir Box
Howard & Co.

New York, New York, 1884
D. 2⅝"

Shallow box for the dressing table with repoussé design of buttercups.
(C)

Private Collection

50-2 Jewelry Casket
Meriden Britannia Company
Meriden, Connecticut, c. 1890
L. 6½"

Oval jewelry box with flat lid and openwork finial. Fixed oval handle
with openwork leaf patterns. Silver-plated. **(C)**

Private Collection

50-3 Jewelry Box
Maker unknown
c. 1915
H. 2¾"

Circular jewelry box with an engine-turned design on the sides and

floral design on the cover. **(C)**

Private Collection

GLOVE BOX.

No. 219. Satin-lined, $72.50, ...

Gold and Oxidized, 13.50, ...

BOUDOIR SET.

THREE PIECES TO MATCH.

HANDKERCHIEF BOX.

JEWEL BOX.

50-4 Boudoir Set
Reed & Barton

Taunton, Massachusetts, c. 1884
L. 12" approx. (glove box)

Matching set of boxes for handkerchiefs, gloves, and jewelry. Each with an engraved design on the sides and a twisted rope finial. Ring handles at the ends. Silver-plated. **(C)**

Reed & Barton catalogue, 1884

50-5 Jewelry Casket
Meriden Britannia Company
Meriden, Connecticut, c. 1886
D. 3"

Cylindrical jewelry box with a rope border at the base, the cover engraved with a floral design. Silver-plated. **(C)**

50-6 Hairpin Box
Webster Mfg. Co.
Brooklyn, New York, c. 1870
L. 4½"

Oval hairpin box on four ball feet. A hairpin in relief on the lid and the legend "A Friend in Need." Border of shells and scrolls. **(C)**

Private Collection

50-7 Glove Box
H. C. Wilcox & Co.
Meriden, Connecticut, c. 1880
L. 13"

Rectangular glove box with a narrow scroll and floral design along the
borders. The center of the lid with a scroll, floral, and leaf-enclosed
monogrammed cartouche. Silver-plated. **(C)**

Private Collection

Acknowledgments

A book that includes as diverse a selection of silver and silver plate as this one must depend on many sources. I am grateful to the many corporations, dealers, and individuals whose assistance was instrumental in compiling this book.

In particular I wish to thank the International Silver Company; the Gorham Division of Textron, Inc.; the Reed & Barton Company; the Towle Silversmiths; the Newark Museum; I. Freeman & Son, Inc.; the De Young Museum; Ren's Antiques; and the Lyndhurst Corporation.

I am most indebted to those collectors who not only allowed their premises to be invaded by a photographer and note taker, but graciously provided them with food and drink as well. Among the great many who deserve thanks are: Vicki Brooks, Mr. and Mrs. William C. Burt, Ulysses Dietz, Sibyl McCormac Groff, Helen Hamilton, David Hanks, Edmund P. Hogan, Jayne Ingram, Soovia Janis, Alice Kimball, Mr. and Mrs. Richard Lim, Mr. and Mrs. Paul S. Lipson, Richard McGeehan, David M.S. Pettigrew, Mr. and Mrs. Theodore Rockafellow, Robert Santangelo, Mrs. Mitchell Specter, Charles W. Thrash, Jr., Alan Voll, Arthur J. Williams, and Janet Yankauer.

Glossary

Acanthus—the leaf of a Mediterranean plant with a large spine and irregular edges; used as a decorative pattern.

Anthemion—a stylized motif based on the classical Greek honeysuckle.

Bail—the handle of a kettle or basket, fitted to its center and from which the utensil hangs; usually moveable.

Beading—a form of decoration used for rims and edges. A row of tiny adjoining balls, like a string of beads.

Bright cut—incised decoration on a silver surface, with broad strokes that reflect light.

Cartouche—an ornamental tablet often used as an engraved decorative motif on silver. A cartouche often encloses a coat of arms, initials, or an inscription.

Cast—silver formed in a mold and applied to the body of a piece.

Chased—decorated by chiseling.

Crenelated—evenly notched or indented.

Die-rolled—narrow ribbons of machined silver used for borders.

Egg-and-dart—decoration of alternating egg and dart shapes.

Embossed—decorated with figures or ornamental relief made by a die or tool upon a smooth surface.

Engraved—incised line decoration.

Etching—surface decoration bitten-in with acid.

Finial—the decorative apex of an object, often used to lift the cover.

Fluted—a surface ornamented by parallel channels or grooves, usually vertical.

Gadrooned—a series of curved, convex ridges, varying in form but joined at their extremities. An abbreviated form is often used on the rim of a vessel.

Matte finish—a dull surface made by delicate, evenly-spaced punchwork.

Medallion—a round or oval disk decorated with heads of figures, usually cast like a coin.

Palmette—classical motif similar to a fan or stylized palm leaf.

Putti—chubby, nude infant children.

Quatrefoil—a leaf or flower design consisting of four equal parts radiating from a common center.

Reeded—a surface ornamented by a series of parallel ridges; the opposite of fluted.

Repoussé—a raised pattern made by beating metal from the reverse side with hammer and punches.

Rococo—elaborate ornamentation of scrolls, shells, etc.

Stippled—engraved with dots to produce an effect of shading.

Strap work—a form of decoration simulating interlaced bands.

Swags—an arrangement of flowers, leaves, or fruit bound together and suspended from a decorative bow knot or classic urn. Also called festoons.

Trefoil—decorative figure composed of three parts.

Treillage—latticework.

Trifid—a handle split into three parts by deep clefts or notches.

Wrythen—spiral fluting.

Selected Bibliography

Buhler, Katherine C. *American Silver*. New York: The World Publishing Co., 1950.

Carpenter, Charles H., Jr., and Carpenter, Mary G. *Tiffany Silver*. New York: Dodd, Mead & Co., 1978.

Fales, Martha Gandy. *Early American Silver*. Excalibur Books.

Hogan, Edmund P. *An American Heritage*. Dallas: Taylor Publishing Company, 1977.

Hood, Graham. *American Silver: A History of Style 1650-1900*. New York, Praeger Publishers, 1971.

McClinton, Katherine Morrison. *Antiques: Past and Present*. New York, Clarkson N. Potter, Inc., 1971.

———. *Collecting American 19th Century Silver*. New York: Charles Scribner's Sons, 1968.

May, Earl Chapin. *A Century of Silver: 1847-1947*. New York: Robert M. McBride & Co., 1947.

Rainwater, Dorothy T. *Encyclopedia of American Silver Manufacturers*. New York: Crown Publishers, Inc., 1975.

Rainwater, Dorothy T., ed. *Sterling Silver Hollowware*. Princeton: The Pyne Press, 1973.

Rainwater, Dorothy T., and Rainwater, H. Ivan. *American Silverplate*. Knoxville, Tennessee: Thomas Nelson and Hanover, Pennsylvania: Everybody's Press, 1968.

Schwartz, Marvin D. *Collector's Guide to Antique American Silver*. New York: Doubleday & Co., 1975.

Stow, Millicent. *American Silver*. New York: M. Barrows and Co., Inc., 1950.

Victorian Silverplated Hollowware. Princeton: The Pyne Press, 1972.

Ward, Barbara McLean, and Gerald, W.R., eds. *Silver in American Life*. Boston: David R. Godine, 1979.

Wenham, Edward. *The Practical Book of American Silver*. Philadelphia and New York: J.B. Lippincott Company, 1949.

Index